THE CLUTTER FIX

THE NO-FAIL, STRESS-FREE GUIDE
TO ORGANIZING YOUR HOME

SHANNON ACHESON

BETHANYHOUSE
a division of Baker Publishing Group
Minneapolis, Minnesota

© 2022 by Shannon Acheson

Published by Bethany House Publishers
11400 Hampshire Avenue South
Minneapolis, Minnesota 55438
www.bethanyhouse.com

Bethany House Publishers is a division of
Baker Publishing Group, Grand Rapids, Michigan

Printed in the United States of America

Library of Congress Cataloging-in-Publication Data
Names: Acheson, Shannon, author.
Title: The clutter fix : the no-fail, stress-free guide to organizing your home / Shannon Acheson.
Description: Minneapolis, Minnesota : Bethany House, a division of Baker Publishing Group, [2022] | Includes index.
Identifiers: LCCN 2022013963 | ISBN 9780764240003 (paperback) | ISBN 9780764241222 (casebound) | ISBN 9781493439171 (ebook)
Subjects: LCSH: Storage in the home. | Orderliness. | House cleaning.
Classification: LCC TX309 .A337 2022 | DDC 648/.8--dc23/eng/20220511
LC record available at https://lccn.loc.gov/2022013963

Unless otherwise indicated, Scripture quotations are from THE HOLY BIBLE, NEW IN-TERNATIONAL VERSION®, NIV® Copyright © 1973, 1978, 1984, 2011 by Biblica, Inc.® Used by permission. All rights reserved worldwide.

Scripture quotations marked ESV are from The Holy Bible, English Standard Version® (ESV®), copyright © 2001 by Crossway, a publishing ministry of Good News Publishers. Used by permission. All rights reserved. ESV Text Edition: 2016

Scripture quotations marked KJV are from the King James Version of the Bible.

Cover design by Studio Gearbox
Cover photography by Shannon Acheson

Author represented by William K. Jensen Literary Agency

Baker Publishing Group publications use paper produced from sustainable forestry practices and post-consumer waste whenever possible.

22 23 24 25 26 27 28   7 6 5 4 3 2 1

"Do you tend to let your home get overly cluttered? Stacks of stuff. Piles of papers. All making you feel defeated. *The Clutter Fix* will become your go-to manual for decisively dealing with all your things. This practical, step-by-step resource will empower you to tackle the task of getting organized so both your home and your mind can finally become calm and chaos-free."

Karen Ehman, Proverbs 31 Ministries national speaker
and Bible teacher, *New York Times* bestselling author
of *Reach Out, Gather In: 40 Days to Opening
Your Heart and Home*, wife, and mom of three

"From the quick wins, to the right mindset, to the action steps and necessary maintenance of your newly decluttered space, Shannon has thought of everything you need! *The Clutter Fix* will guide you through the mess so you can find the peaceful home you've always wanted."

—Melissa Michaels, *New York Times* bestselling author

"I can't tell you how many times I've thought to myself, *Oh, I'm such a NOSO*. The part of Shannon's organizing philosophy that involves identifying your decluttering and organizing styles is so brilliant and has led to so much harmony and understanding in my home."

—Courtenay Hartford, author, *The Cleaning Ninja*

"Shannon shares practical, easy-to-follow decluttering strategies for everyone, no matter your personality, experience, or clutter level. I love how her faith and encouraging demeanor are evident throughout the book. It feels like she's right beside you cheering you on as you go through the decluttering process!"

—Abby Lawson, organizing expert, Abby Organizes

"As a mom of five and lifelong disorganized Creative Bargain Hunter (my clutter duo-personality), I appreciate Shannon's practical and grace-filled suggestions on how to achieve immediate organizational wins in my life. She's a wonderful cheerleader and coach, with her detailed lists giving me just the right amount of push I need."

—Jen Schmidt, author, *Just Open the Door*; founder of Balancing
Beauty and Bedlam and The Becoming Conference

Once again, this book is
for my husband and best friend, Dean,
and our three kiddos,
Jonah, Lillian, and Megan.
Home is *always* wherever I am with you.

Acknowledgments

First, thank you to my heavenly Father for everything you've done in my life, even before I actually knew and loved you. I can't even imagine how different my life would be without you.

Thank you to Dean and our kiddos for being so supportive of me and what I've been called to. You guys are THE BEST cheerleaders, and I will love you and cheer *you* on in *your* endeavors forever.

And thank you to Bethany House, Jennifer Dukes Lee, and the entire BHP team for believing in me and asking me if I'd like to write a second book—this book you're now holding in your hands. Thank you to Teresa Evenson for once again walking me through the book deal process.

You have all helped to make my dreams of being an author come true over the last few years. Thank you from the bottom of my heart.

Contents

#THECLUTTERFIX

Your Decluttering Game Plan

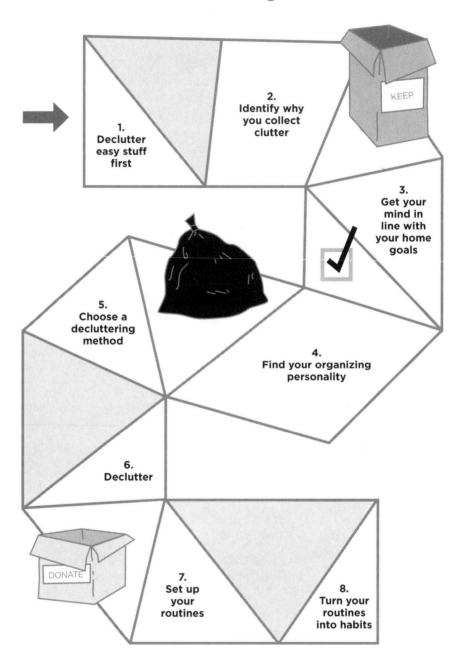

1. Declutter easy stuff first

2. Identify why you collect clutter

KEEP

3. Get your mind in line with your home goals

5. Choose a decluttering method

4. Find your organizing personality

6. Declutter

DONATE

7. Set up your routines

8. Turn your routines into habits

Introduction &
How to Use
The Clutter Fix

Hey there, lovely home-makin' friend. I'm so glad you picked up *The Clutter Fix*! If you desperately want your home to be a calm, peaceful breath of fresh air, you *need* to read this book.

I'm Shannon. Wife to my best friend, not-so-traditional home-schooling momma, veteran blogger, author, designer, and ever-thankful child of God. I believe that **home is the most important place on earth.** In my first book, *Home Made Lovely*, I mentioned that there is something *almost* indescribable about the longing we all feel deep down for home. We desire it to be our safe place, our refuge, our retreat, and our soft place to land. It's where we instinctively want to go to recharge our drained batteries and to reconnect with our family. Home can be a place of great ministry to the world around us too when we use it to love on our family, friends, and neighbors. Jesus even used home as an analogy for heaven when He said, "My Father's house has many rooms" (John 14:2). Our homes have a huge impact on our lives and our well-being, and with more people working and doing school from home in the last few years, the impact of the home on our lives is even greater than before.

I've been told that my superpower is breaking big things down into simple, easy-to-follow, step-by-step processes. Using this technique, I teach all sorts of ways to make our homes lovely on my blog, in my books, through other websites and publications, and via virtual classes. This includes meal plans that save time, DIY projects that save money, Bible verses that help you sleep better, and decorating strategies to suit your family's real life. My aim in creating all these how-to's is to equip women, especially mommas of all ages and stages, with the skills and tools they need to create the home they've always wanted, right where they are.

As I've done this, I've asked thousands of women what their *biggest home issue* is. The answer is most often *clutter*. Repeatedly, women have told me that they feel overwhelmed, lack confidence, feel depressed, and are generally unsure of where to begin tackling the mess in their homes. The clutter and disorganization leave them feeling "chaotic," like they are "spinning their wheels," and keep them from "focusing on being a good wife and mom." Others have even said that they are "sometimes embarrassed to open the front door."[1] And I'm not the only one hearing this. Shelley Davies, a Vancouver-based decluttering expert, says, "The words I'm hearing over and over again are 'I'm drowning' or 'I'm suffocating.'"[2] An article in the *Vancouver Sun* goes on to say, "The never-ending stream of clothing, dollar-store gizmos, seasonal decor, gifts, paperwork, sentimental items, unfinished projects and overloaded Billy bookcases is just too much."[3]

Does any of that sound familiar, my friend? If so, you are definitely *not* alone. "According to the Professional Organizers of Canada, 83% of Canadians indicate they are extremely disorganized, and 91% feel clutter negatively affects their lives."[4] The US has equally dismal numbers: "Fifty percent of Americans say they feel overwhelmed by the amount of stuff in their homes, with the average American household having 42 items they're no longer using (that's more than 5.3 billion items)."[5]

Amazingly, all these feelings of overwhelm and stress tied to clutter are explainable by science: "According to *Psychology Today*, **clutter causes stress in part because of its excessive visual stimuli. It also signals to our brains that our work is never done and creates**

Definition of Decluttering: Decluttering is the stuff you don't need leaving your house.[6]

Definition of Organizing: Organizing is creating a specific home for everything you own.

A lived-in house will still have messes. Those messes will just be so much easier to tidy up once you've decluttered and organized.

guilt, anxiety, and the feeling of being overwhelmed."[7] According to a UCLA study, women who see their home as cluttered have a higher level of the stress hormone cortisol.[8] That is the fight-or-flight hormone, the one that plays an important role in keeping us safe in a crisis. It's also the hormone that when elevated for long periods of time, such as in a constantly cluttered environment, can cause anxiety, depression, headaches, heart disease, trouble sleeping, and—*joy of all joys,* weight gain.

Clutter isn't just about the stuff. It's about how we feel in our homes and how we live out our lives. It's mental and emotional, not just physical. It's about being good stewards of the time and resources God has given us. When I asked the same women who told me they were overwhelmed by their clutter how they would feel if they could get their clutter chaos under control, they said that a weight would be lifted, they would be able to handle life better, and they would be able to breathe again. Isn't that how we all want to feel in our homes— *lighter, full of energy, and more organized?*

The Bible says: "My people will live in peaceful dwelling places, in secure homes, in undisturbed places of rest" (Isaiah 32:18). Through *The Clutter Fix,* I will help you create those undisturbed places of rest in your home here on earth while you await your real home in heaven. Throughout these pages, I hope to encourage you mightily as I show you how to:

- Make near-instant progress with a few quick wins via small decluttering projects that feel big, to give you a big boost of encouragement to keep going.

- Identify why you collect clutter—your Clutter Personality—so that, going forward, you can stop the clutter before it enters your home.
- Discover your Organizing Personality, which will help determine which decluttering and organizational methods work best for *you*. Because, unlike the premise of the "spark joy" teaching, decluttering and organizing is *not* always a one-size-fits-all solution.
- Deal with sentimental items, and the fear and guilt that are often felt when parting with hand-me-downs and heirlooms.
- Get your family onboard with your decluttering and organizing—or maybe *not*.
- Declutter each and every room and space in your home, from the garage to the attic, with clear, concise, step-by-step instructions.
- Maintain a clutter-free home with the secret weapons of rhythms, routines, and the awesome power of habits.

Plus, I'm going to share one hundred and twenty things you can quickly clear out of your home without any guilt or stress so that you gain even more confidence in your decluttering abilities. *Buh-bye, elevated cortisol levels—hello, big deep breath of fresh air!*

Things You Should Know before You Read *The Clutter Fix*

There are a few things I think you should know before you further delve into *The Clutter Fix* and use it to tackle the clutter in your home. **First of all, I'm just me.** I'm a momma of three grown (or almost grown) kiddos whom I homeschooled via one method or another for *years*. I work from home, and there are five people and one wee doggie living under our roof. I'm an author, a blogger, and a decorator. Given all that, it's safe to say I know messes, clutter, *and* organization well. But I am not a *professional* organizer. I am basing everything I share here on my own personal experience and from years of figuring things out in our home, as well as feedback from my awesome blog readers, and from studying decluttering and organizing experts online.

I address women specifically throughout the book because that's who I tend to speak to the most. But I'm a big believer that everyone—of an appropriate age—who lives in a home should take part in caring for it. That means hubbies, kids, and all. If you're not a woman, that's okay. Awesome, even. You can still use what I'm teaching here.

I quote Bible verses. I am a Bible-believing, born-again Christian. Which means I quote the Bible from time to time in my books and online. However, I am not a biblical scholar or a theology student, nor do I speak any of the original languages the Bible was written in. It is *never* my intention to steer you wrong, but if I do get the context wrong with a verse I quote, please forgive me. My goal is to serve you and help you to understand and learn from what I write. Which brings me to . . .

Take from this book what you need and leave the rest. If you feel like something doesn't line up with your beliefs (as a Christian or not), feel free to just move along to the next part of the book. I think we've all forgotten that we don't have to agree 100% with everything someone says in order to glean some good knowledge from them (or to be friends with them or to sit down for a meal with them, for that matter). There will be times when you will nod your head excitedly in agreement with what I say, and there may be other times when you vehemently shake it back and forth because you think I'm bonkers. That's okay. Please take and use what you feel will work for you and simply discard the rest. This is not a primary theological discussion or a life-and-death decision. You do not have to agree with everything I say to use some of what I say to make your home more peaceful and clutter-free. Make sense?

Some things you read here may seem a bit familiar. Ecclesiastes 1:9 says (in part), "There is nothing new under the sun." There are many authors, professional organizers, designers, and otherwise talented people who have come before me. They have shared some fabulous ideas, and I share a few snippets or quotes from them here in

The Clutter Fix. That doesn't mean I agree with or endorse everything they have ever said or will say, but rather I want to use their words and knowledge that I share here to further highlight what I'm teaching you. My intent is to give you a full body of work that will help you to get a handle on the clutter in your home once and for all. If you find that I've missed giving credit anywhere, I apologize profusely, and please let me know.

But I'm also going to share fresh, new ideas that actually work. In *The Clutter Fix*, we're going deep into the thoughts and feelings behind clutter and organizing, as well as into the step-by-step process for each and every space in your home. We will address the head, the heart, and the practical all together as a way to tackle your clutter and tame your home. I'm giving you *all* the tools you need to carve out a calm and peaceful, clutter-free dwelling place.

There is no magic bullet. I'm hesitant to say this because I don't want to put you off, but I think we've collectively gotten a little lazy in our homes over the last several years, and our expectations are *definitely* a little skewed. We *are* genuinely busy and overscheduled. But everywhere I look, I see exhausted mommas searching for some instant, one-step solution that will take care of their clutter, organization, and even their cooking and cleaning routines. We think that if we just find that *one thing*, we won't have to work at maintaining a lovely home ever again. We won't have to contend with the mountains of laundry or the dishes that our family uses on a daily basis. Sister, that's just not how it works. A true home—one that is lived in and actively used—will require maintenance and work *on the regular*. If you're a Bible-believing Christian, like I am, you know that God created the world in six days and rested for only one, and He shared this in Genesis as a model for us to follow. Unfortunately, books like *The 4-Hour Work Week* and the current expectations of instant gratification in everything (hello Instacart, Prime One-Day Delivery, Disney+ streaming, and so on) can confuse us and make us think we shouldn't have to work at things as much as we actually do. Can we streamline things and make our lives and homes easier to manage? ABSOLUTELY, without question. And I'm going to help you do that here. But can we forego tidying and cleaning forever after because we do it once or think there's some elusive fix? Nope, I'm afraid not.

I am not a psychologist, psychiatrist, or therapist. When I talk about the psychology behind clutter or how we feel in our homes, it's because some people need hard facts or science and aren't as "feely" as I am. I tend to learn something experientially and then go and find a professional or expert to quote to add to my knowledge. Think of it like a school essay, where I would include my point of view and opinions, but I am required to back them up with sources. *In this way, I'm sharing both head and heart knowledge with you.*

This book contains lots of information broken down in an easily understandable way. **There are many worksheets and checklists.** These resources will help guide you through your home's decluttering and organizing process. And give you a sense of accomplishment when you check things off as you complete them. Plus, I kinda have a thing for lists! The goal here is to get excess stuff out of the house and help you keep it out. To find an organizational rhythm that works for you and your home, so that you can feel light and peaceful instead of burdened and frazzled. I've even created more checklists and tools for you outside of what I could fit here. Just go to HomeMadeLovely.com /tcfbonus to download them. I highly recommend that you make use of these tools to help you in your decluttering and organizing journey.

This book is for the person who is ready to declutter and organize. I created it to help *you* get a handle on the clutter in your home. I'm assuming, since you're the one reading it, that you're the one who manages the most home stuff in your household. I didn't write it so you could change your spouse, kids, parents, or in-laws—even though I really think that they should be open to the changes you're making and want to help ease any burden that you feel from clutter. Read that again, lovely. This book is for *you*, to help *you*, not necessarily to change others around you. I'll talk about how you may be able to get your family on board in a little while. But *The Clutter Fix* is for *you*, my friend. You can only change your own behaviors and expectations. The sooner you accept this, the better the whole decluttering and organizing process (and dare I say, your life) will be. And maybe, just maybe, your family and friends will see how much happier you are with less stuff, and they'll come alongside you in this journey too.

I do not know your life specifics. I don't know your history or your story. **I can't solve all your problems.** I don't know with complete certainty why you collect clutter, or how you best organize. But this book, this guidebook I've lovingly poured my heart into, will help you get a handle on your home no matter what your life looks like or why you have all that stuff. These steps work for me in my home and for others whose lives do not look like mine. And they will help you too.

I am not judging you, and I encourage you not to judge yourself too harshly either. A cluttered home can feel like an embarrassment, and people sometimes feel ashamed because they've let things get out of control. This is often followed by a lack of confidence. But darling, your home's current cluttered and messy state is entirely fixable *if you want to fix it*. If you are looking to make changes, I will mightily cheer you on as you make progress in reaching your home decluttering and organizing goals. Today is a new day, I believe in you, and you can totally do this.

This is not Instagram or one of those Netflix shows filled with pretty or inspirational photos of perfectly organized, color-coded spaces. I love pretty pictures as much as anyone. Honestly, lovely spaces are kinda my thing. And beautifully organized cupboards and drawers? Be still my heart. This just isn't the place for that. *The Clutter Fix* is meant to be a handbook and an instruction manual, not eye candy. You are meant to dive in and actually use the step-by-step instructions, worksheets, and checklists to declutter and organize *your* home. Whether it ends up looking like those inspiration spaces you love or not, the goal is to make progress. Baby steps. One foot in front of the other until you look back and are in awe of how far you have come.

You may need to read this book more than once. Even though I've said that we're getting rid of your clutter and *keeping* it out for good, life happens. And clutter happens as life happens sometimes. It's okay. Just take a deep breath and pick up where you left off when you can or flip to the specific section that applies when you need to tackle or re-tackle a space.

The steps for decluttering and organizing each space are essentially the same. As I said, there is no magic bullet. But I outline each step for each room, one by one, so that you can flip to a specific page and work on any room in your home at any time. (This will be even easier if you grab the free printable tabs at HomeMadeLovely.com /tcfbonus that denote the sections and chapters in *The Clutter Fix*.) By the end of the book, after lots of repetition, you should have the steps practically memorized, which is kinda the point . . . to help you get to a place where decluttering and organizing is done on autopilot, with little to no stress at all.

How to Use The Clutter Fix

There are three main parts (aside from the quick wins tools in part 1) in creating a decluttered home:

1. Getting your *mindset* cleaned up when it comes to clutter and habits
2. The initial *purge* when you're getting started clearing out the accumulated clutter
3. *Maintenance mode,* where you set up systems and habits to help you keep up with the management of your stuff

Whether you choose to utilize the quick wins tools in chapters 1 and 2 or not, you need to get into your headspace and understand why you collect clutter in the first place. An understanding of why clutter accumulates in your home will help you *prevent it from happening in the future.* I'm going to help you with this. I will also help you deal with the tough stuff, like sentimental clutter and how to get your family on board, in part 2. Make use of the affirmations that I've included to help you reset the way that you think about clutter and your home. (If affirmations sound woo-woo to you, I promise you that the way we're going to use them here, they're not. Read chapter 8 so you understand where I'm coming from and how helpful they can be.)

To successfully have a clutter-free home, you obviously need to declutter your stuff. One blogger defines decluttering success as "stuff I don't need leaving my house."[9] It's time to purge all the excess that's taken over your home, little by little over the last however-many months, years, or decades. To help you do this, after we've got your head in line with your goals, I'm going to walk you through clearing out the clutter from every room and every space in your home one room and one step at a time in part 3. I'll show you how to keep only what you need and love, and/or things that serve a specific purpose in your home and life. Then I'm going to show you how to gracefully and peacefully let go of the rest with specifics for each room, handy checklists, and other tools that will help you. And I will also help you organize the things you are keeping in a pleasing and orderly fashion that works for *you* and your Organizing Personality.

> **"Your home is a living space, not a storage space."**
>
> —FRANCINE JAY

And finally, I'm going to teach you how to create rhythms and routines in part 4—*Master Maintenance Mode*, aka living everyday life. In maintenance mode, *after* you've purged and everything has its place, you will create and implement rhythms and routines that will serve you and your home goals. I will give you sample routines and teach you how to create your own habits that will enable you to stay on top of things and keep your home tidy with as little effort as possible so that you can have that peaceful, lovely home to savor and enjoy. Which is the point of this whole process, right?

In *The Power of Habit*, Charles Duhigg says, "Everyone goes through periods when we know we need to change. Studies, however, tell us that simply *knowing* often isn't enough. Sometimes it takes something else—exposure to the right idea, hearing stories that resonate in our own lives, a certain kind of encouragement—that makes the first step feel within reach."[10] I pray that through *The Clutter Fix* I can be the encouragement that helps the first few steps of creating a more peaceful home feel within reach for you.

If you've been dealing with the clutter chaos in your home by pretending your space doesn't affect your mood—but you know it does; if you're telling yourself that you'll get to it someday, which you and I both know is just another way of saying never; if you've lost confidence in yourself to do anything about the clutter because you've tried all the decluttering methods before and they just didn't work, then this book is for you.

Because you are so much closer to a clutter-free, organized home than you know, lovely, and you can get there, one step at a time.

A Quick Clutter Assessment

1. How does your home currently feel?

   _____

   _____

2. Does it feel like your peaceful, organized happy place?

   ☐ Yes   ☐ No

3. Does everything you own have an assigned home?

   ☐ Yes   ☐ No

4. Can you tidy your spaces and rooms in ten minutes or less?

   ☐ Yes   ☐ No

5. Does your home feel a little more chaotic and scattered than you'd like it to?

   ☐ Yes   ☐ No

6. Are you always forgetting where your keys/glasses/remote are?

   ☐ Yes   ☐ No

7. Is your counter piled high with papers with no end to the stack in sight?

   ☐ Yes   ☐ No

8. What are your top three reasons for decluttering?

   _____

   _____

   _____

9. On a scale of 1–10, how confident do you feel about decluttering your home? (1 = not at all confident, 10 = very confident)

   1   2   3   4   5   6   7   8   9   10

10. Describe how cluttered each of the following is in your home currently and then describe how you'd like it to be:

Front Porch _____

_____

Entryway _____

_____

Dining Room _____

_____

Living/Family Room _____

_____

Kitchen _____

_____

Bathroom _____

_____

Bedroom _____

_____

Linen Closet _____

_____

Laundry Room _____

_____

Playroom _____

_____

Home Office _____

_____

Basement/Attic _____

_____

Garage _____

_____

11. How do you want your home to feel? This is actually a question I ask my Decorating Uncomplicated students in the very first lesson. Because how you want your home to *feel* is where you start turning your house into the home you've always wanted. Our brains are wired to hold on to feelings and emotions. And for any lasting change to happen, you need to feel the emotion behind the end result. You need to know your *why* and how that specifically feels for you, in your home.

    List three feelings you currently have about your cluttered home and how you would like to feel about it instead:

Current feelings	**Goal feelings**

12. Use the space below to describe what your *life* would look like if your home was clutter-free right now.

_____

_____

_____

_____

_____

_____

_____

Next, you're going to get a jump start on your decluttering with some small wins that feel big.

PART 1

GET SOME QUICK WINS UNDER YOUR BELT

CHAPTER 1

The 10-Day Decluttering Shortcut

I decided to put these quick wins and decluttering hacks at the very beginning of the book because if you make use of them now, they will give you the confidence to tackle bigger, more complicated clutter later.

Obviously, I want to see you do the full home decluttering. To get *all* your stuff under control. To read *The Clutter Fix* from start to finish, so that you can also *keep* your home clutter-free. But I want to give you not just *words* of encouragement, but also a concrete feeling of accomplishment and a *deep knowing* that you can do it. You *can* declutter and make massive progress in your home.

So, if you're feeling like you can't get a handle on your clutter, or that you've tried to get your home clutter-free and failed before, use these next two decluttering hacks, The 10-Day Decluttering Shortcut, and the list of 120 Things to Throw Away—*Guilt-Free* as stepping-stones. These hacks will help you *immediately* improve the spaces in your home—at the same time giving you confidence in your own abilities to handle the clutter. You *can* do this. Your home can be clutter-free and that wonderfully lovely space that you and your family need and deserve. Repeat after me: *"I can declutter and organize my home."*

The 10-Day Decluttering Shortcut

In this ten-day shortcut, I'm going to help you clear the clutter out of the two highest-traffic areas of your home—the entryway and some very specific clutter-collecting areas of the kitchen—so that you get a much-needed quick win in your battle against clutter.

There's nothing quite like coming home to a neat and tidy space. "Getting rid of excess stuff can benefit your mental health by making you feel calmer, happier, and more in control. A tidier space can make for a more relaxed mind."[1] So let's tidy your way to more calm and relaxation, shall we?

What You'll Need:

- The 10-Day Decluttering Shortcut instructions (that would be what you're reading now)
- Pencil/pen
- Garbage bags
- Recycling bin
- Masking tape and marker to label donation bags vs. garbage bags
- Paper shredder (optional)
- Broom and dustpan or vacuum cleaner
- Mop
- A dishcloth and all-purpose cleaner spray (or water)

Ready to get started? Here's a high-level overview of the spaces we're going to tackle in the next ten days:

1. Tidy the front entryway
2. Clean out the front hall closet

3. Reduce the incoming paper
4. Stop the junk-mail clutter in its tracks
5. Clean off the outside of your fridge
6. Clean out the pantry
7. Deal with the junk drawer
8. Purge all the other kitchen drawers
9. Purge the kitchen cabinets
10. Clear off the counters

> **A decluttered home matters because**
>
> "I find I function better with organized and clean spaces."

Take a deep breath and dive in. As you go through the 10-Day Decluttering Shortcut, as well as the remainder of the book, I encourage you to share your progress on social media using the hashtag #theclutterfix!

Day 1—Tidy the Front Entryway

To kick off this 10-Day Decluttering Shortcut, we're going to start with one of the most highly trafficked areas in your home . . . the entryway. In fact, we're going to spend a couple of days in this space because it's so important. It's the first impression visitors get of the inside of your home. It's also the first space *you* experience when you walk in your front door. So, it should totally work for you!

To begin, stand in your entryway for a few minutes and take a good look around you. What do you see? Does what you see make you feel stressed or unhappy? Or does it fill you with peace and calm? If your entryway is perfectly tidy and organized and you feel at peace with its current state, feel free to jump ahead a couple of days in the shortcut. If it's stress you feel, take a deep breath, beautiful, and don't panic. We're going to whip this space into shape in next to no time at all.

> **"Once a small win has been accomplished, forces are set in motion that favor another small win."**
>
> —CHARLES DUHIGG

Tidy your entryway the easy way:

☐ Quickly gather any and all garbage that you can see at a glance. Toss it immediately. Now, look for broken-beyond-repair umbrellas or dog leashes, anything that long ago lost its mate, like mittens or flip-flops, and toss those too.

☐ Next, grab another garbage bag and collect any pieces you know are too small or not being worn anymore. Label this bag with masking tape and a marker, and set it aside to donate at the end of the ten-day shortcut. If you come across something that's not being used currently because it's for the wrong season, tuck it into the closet to deal with tomorrow.

☐ Gather things that belong elsewhere in the house into a box. Put them away as soon as you've sorted everything in the entryway today.

☐ Now, put everything into the closet that doesn't belong out for daily use. It's called a coat closet for a reason. We'll deal with it tomorrow.

☐ Give any tables, lamps, or artwork a quick dusting, and then do a quick sweep of the floor with the broom and maybe a quick mopping, and you're done.

Voilà! A clean and tidy entryway!

☐ Day 1 complete

Day 2—Clean Out the Front Hall Closet

Now that your entryway itself is neat and tidy and clutter-free, we're going to clear the clutter out of the front hall closet. (Technically, you could tackle both the entry and the closet in the same day if you want, but it is often helpful to start small when decluttering, especially if you're already feeling overwhelmed.)

Since we've already taken the time to declutter the entry, we're going to empty the closet into the next closest room to the entry. For us, that would be the dining room. For you, it may be the same or it may be another room or a hallway.

Here are the hall closet decluttering steps:

- ☐ Empty the entire closet.
- ☐ Immediately toss anything that doesn't have a match, can't be salvaged, or is obviously trash.
- ☐ Gather things that don't belong in the closet into a box and set it aside.
- ☐ Now gather the items that don't fit or don't get worn anymore. You may need to grab kiddos to have them try things on for this step. Once you've determined something doesn't fit, put it in the donate bag you started yesterday. Continue until you have only the good stuff remaining.

> "A huge body of research has shown that small wins have enormous power, an influence disproportionate to the accomplishments of the victories themselves."
>
> —CHARLES DUHIGG

- ☐ While the closet is empty, give it a good dusting and a sweeping. Mop the floor if needed. Use a Magic Eraser to get rid of any scuff marks or fingerprints. You can even touch up any chipped or peeling paint if you really want to and you have the time to do so.
- ☐ Sort everything that remains either by season or by person.
- ☐ If you need new hangers, storage baskets, or shoe shelves, measure your closet space carefully and then go get them. (Or wait until we cover Organizing Personalities in chapter 5 and do it then.)

☐ Return everything neatly to the closet, hanging what needs hanging and lining shoes and boots up beneath those. At our house, our front hall closet is divided in two by a hanging set of shoe cubbies, and we keep the kids' stuff on one side and my husband Dean's and my stuff on the other. And then we sort each side by season, with the items needed for the current season most easily reachable from the doorway and the out-of-season items tucked further in.

☐ Now go put away the items that belong elsewhere.

Wahoo! You've completed day 2 and your entryway is lookin' fine!

☐ Day 2 complete

Day 3—Reduce the Incoming Paper

Paper clutter is a huge problem in many homes, and day 3 of this ten-day challenge begins the satisfying journey of eliminating the paper clutter in your house.

To get a handle on paper clutter, you first need to reduce the amount of paper that comes into your home to begin with, so it doesn't continue to pile up.

So, if you have a paper pile sitting around as most people do, you need to go get it. Then:

☐ Go through the paper pile and sort it into three piles—bills, junk mail, and other (birthday cards, family letters, etc.).

☐ Set the junk-mail pile aside for tomorrow and the other pile for later when we tackle more paper clutter in chapter 12.

☐ Focusing on the bills pile, go through and sort the papers by the billing company. If you've ignored this for a while, you may have a lot of sorting to do. Then stack them all together. Because I run a business from home and I'm mostly a Nothing Out + Simple Organizer (more on Organizing Personalities in chapter 5) when it comes to paperwork, I keep all the utility bills together for tax purposes. But you sort your pile however you need to for your home.

☐ Now hop on your computer with your sorted bills stacked in front of you, go through the pile, and sign up for each company's digital/online billing as you go. Be sure to use an email address whose inbox the bills won't get lost in or ignored.

☐ Now, file the paper bills that need keeping (say, for tax purposes or reference), and shred and toss those you don't need to keep. If you don't have a filing system set up yet, just sort your bills into appropriate file folders and put them somewhere safe for now. Like I said, we'll get to more paper-clutter organization later.

Going forward, when each bill arrives in your inbox, you can either

- open it and pay it immediately, or
- favorite/star the email in your inbox or file it in its own folder and add the amount owing to your budget spreadsheet. Then pay it when the time comes to do your banking each week/month.

Yay, you! You've gotten a head start on tackling your paper clutter!

☐ Day 3 complete

Day 4—Stop the Junk-Mail Clutter in Its Tracks

The second step to getting a handle on paper clutter is to stop all the junk-mail clutter that can pile up.
To do this:

☐ Grab the junk mail pile from yesterday.
☐ Sort it by pure junk mail (unsolicited flyers and coupons) and catalogs you've requested.

- ☐ Go through the catalogs quickly. If you've marked any pages in them of items you want or things you want to remember, take a photo of those pages with your phone. Then move those photos into their own folder or album on your phone so you don't lose them.
- ☐ Now go online and unsubscribe from any catalogs or companies that you opted in to receive mail from. You can do this piece by piece individually, or you can Google how to unsubscribe from junk mail using a bulk unsubscribe service. You don't need to keep the physical catalogs because everything can be found online now.
- ☐ Add a note to your physical mailbox that says, "No fliers" or "No junk mail." Etsy has some decals for this if you'd like something prettier. You could also make your own with a cutting machine like a Cricut or Silhouette. This works for community mailboxes too if you put a note inside your individual locked box.
- ☐ Now take that pile of junk mail and catalogs and recycle it!

If any junk mail does make its way into your house after this, make sure to check that your "no junk mail" mailbox note is still in place and simply toss the offending paper into the recycling bin immediately. Commit to not letting it sit around in a pile anymore! #nomore procrastinating

Yippee! You've made huge progress in keeping paper clutter out of your home!

- ☐ Day 4 complete

Day 5—Clean Off the Outside of Your Fridge

Whether it's kids' artwork, coupons, Post-it notes reminding you to buy milk, or save-the-dates, another place that paper and clutter tend to accumulate and become an eyesore is the front and sides of the fridge. But the good news is that it's easy to fix this clutter hotspot!

- ☐ Begin by removing any notices that have expired, whose event date has passed, or that are otherwise totally unnecessary to keep. Recycle them or toss them.
- ☐ Now gather any family photos or snapshots and put them away in an album or photo box or commit to having them framed to display properly. At our house we actually tack the most recent shots—like nieces and nephews' school photos—inside a cabinet door in the kitchen. That way we can still see them every time we open the cupboard door, but they aren't cluttering up the outside of the fridge. And when a new photo arrives, we file the old one away.
- ☐ Next, remove random notes and Post-it's for things you need to remember to buy. Order yourself a list pad that has a magnet on the back and jot things there as you run out. This simplifies and streamlines your shopping list. This you can put on the side of the fridge, for less visual mess on the front of the fridge. Or begin to keep a digital shopping list. You can even share these with family members so they can add items as they need them, and everyone can see what's needed when they're out at the store.
- ☐ Now tackle kids' artwork. Remove what is currently on the fridge and sort it. Implement a rule that if the fridge is where their art will be displayed, rather than elsewhere, each child gets to display one piece at a time. Consider buying one magnetic clip for each child that will hold a few pieces of paper. That way, their art can be rotated, and each child can choose what to display at any time. This also allows them to add a piece to "their spot" as soon as they finish it—without adding more paper clutter to the fridge! When the accumulated artwork gets to be too heavy for the magnet, remove some of the older art to be put away for longer-term storage. I'll talk more

about finished art and memorabilia boxes later. (Be careful to choose magnets with nice smooth edges so they don't scratch your fridge's finish. Ask me how I know that one!)

☐ Toss or put away any extra magnets to avoid more clutter being added.

Wahoo! The front and sides of the fridge are neat and tidy! Step back and notice how nice the kitchen is feeling already, just by clearing that one space!

☐ Day 5 complete

Day 6—Clean Out the Pantry

Whether you have a pantry or just cabinets for your food, it likely gets messy regularly. Which makes sense, since food items are likely rotated through it very frequently—especially if you have teenagers or young adults living in the house, like we do. But it can be really frustrating to try to find anything when you're doing meal prep if the pantry is a disaster. A tidy pantry needs occasional maintenance and organization, but we'll get to that in chapter 12. Here we're just going to get it cleared out.

☐ To begin your pantry decluttering, quickly look through everything while it's still in the pantry and toss anything that has expired or is past its "best before" date.

☐ Next, do a quick look through the pantry again and grab anything your family no longer eats (due to new dislikes or food sensitivities), and put those items into a donation box for the food bank, a local neighbor, or someone else in need. Drop that off when you're finished here.

☐ Now, pull out the remaining items, one type at a time for sorting:

- Take out all the canned goods and sort them on the counter into types of food.
- Then do the same for the boxed and packaged goods.

> **"Out of clutter, find simplicity."**
>
> —ALBERT EINSTEIN

- ☐ Once you have everything pulled out and sorted, wipe down the pantry shelves. Then put everything back in, sorted by type and also by how often you use it—less frequently used items go higher up, more frequently used items in an easier-to-reach location. You can use baskets, bins, and can sorters if you wish (more on storage items that will work for your Organizing Personality in chapter 5).

Way to go! You've created another clutter-free space!

☐ Day 6 complete

Day 7—Deal with the Junk Drawer

Everyone seems to have a junk drawer, most often in the kitchen. It's where we tend to put all the things that don't otherwise have a home, or we're not quite sure what to do with.

At our house, we had one too for the longest time. I think this was just because my family did when I was growing up. But I must tell you, when we finally cleaned ours out in early 2021 and only kept necessary things in it—and gave them each a proper assigned home in the drawer—our kitchen instantly felt less cluttered.

To deal with your junk drawer:

- ☐ Empty the whole thing out onto the counter. Yup, the whole thing. It's gonna be ugly, but only temporarily.
- ☐ Toss any garbage right away. If you're anything like me, this could be seed packets, plant tags, broken elastics, expired

coupons, takeout menus (you really don't need these since they can be found online these days), and anything else that you no longer need. Garbage is garbage. Just let it go, lovely.

☐ Now sort what's left, like with like. Markers with markers, scissors with scissors, tools with tools, etc. Just make simple piles on the counters.

☐ Ask yourself if any of the sorted items belong elsewhere in the house. If they do, put them aside to put away as soon as you're finished with the junk drawer. For example, I keep a couple of basic tools in the kitchen that are mine and used frequently for things like hanging photos or tightening a knob. But I don't keep hubby's tools in the kitchen. So, if any—*heaven forbid!*—had made their way to the junk drawer, I would need to return them to the garage at this point.

☐ Look at what's left that truly belongs nowhere else in your house. We now keep a small set of tools, matches, a lighter, thumbtacks, scissors, and extra keys in our junk drawer.

☐ What small bins or drawer organizers would help keep what's left sorted in the drawer? The things we kept each have their own tray (tools, scissors, matches) or a sealed small container (thumbtacks, keys) that we picked up at the dollar store.

☐ Vacuum and wipe down the inside of the drawer, and then place the things that belong neatly inside.

☐ Vow not to toss anything in there that doesn't belong ever again! (This is much easier to do if there are smaller organizers inside the drawer that prevent things from just getting tossed in.)

Yay! Your junk drawer is finally all neatly dealt with! Maybe it's time to name it something other than junk drawer, like maybe Bob. ;) I kid.

☐ Day 7 complete

Day 8—Purge All the Other Kitchen Drawers

Because they tend to operate on the out-of-sight, out-of-mind principle, kitchen drawers can easily become a dumping ground for duplicates and extras you just don't need to keep.

To clean out your kitchen drawers:

- ☐ Start with the worst drawer (after the junk drawer) and empty everything out onto the counter.
- ☐ Sort like with like. All the serving spoons together, all the spatulas, can openers, tongs, measuring spoons, or whatever is in the drawer you're working on.
- ☐ Toss any items that are melted, damaged, not working, or broken. They are not doing you any good sitting in the drawer taking up space.
- ☐ Get rid of duplicates. If you have two manual can openers, it's very unlikely you will ever need both. If they both work, donate whichever one you don't use.
- ☐ Also, get rid of kitchen tools that don't serve more than one purpose. Like a melon baller or an avocado slicer. A spoon or knife would work just as well. The exception is if you literally use those single-purpose tools daily and they truly make your regular life easier. Like our garlic press. I use that thing at least once a day, most days twice. It's a lifesaver for me. But if your family doesn't eat as much garlic as we do, then a garlic press is unnecessary for you! And if you keep that sort of thing, it ends up cluttering your space and causing unnecessary stress.
- ☐ Before you put everything back in the drawer, give the drawer a good vacuuming to get rid of crumbs and then wipe it down with a damp cloth too.
- ☐ If you need organizers, measure the drawer carefully and go get them. Then return the items to the drawers in an organized fashion.
- ☐ Repeat for each drawer, until you've purged and cleaned them all.

Now all your kitchen drawers are organized and clutter-free!

☐ Day 8 complete

Day 9—Purge the Kitchen Cabinets

Much like with kitchen drawers, the "out of sight, out of mind" mentality often prevails with closed-door kitchen cabinets too. But clutter behind closed doors is still clutter, and it messes with your mind and disrupts the peace in your home.
To purge the kitchen cabinets:

☐ Open and empty one or two at a time. Chances are you have a couple of cupboards that contain similar things. For example, we have two places that contain our plastic reusable food containers, mixing bowls, and water bottles. So, I'd empty and sort those at the same time because things could go back in either spot, depending on how they fit.

☐ Toss (or recycle if possible) any pieces that have lost their lids or that are broken. You could consider using small containers that no longer have a lid or whose lid is broken as organizers for other drawers and cupboards.

☐ Set aside (in one spot) any pieces you haven't used in six months or more. This applies to pots and pans, food storage containers, and small appliances too. Then decide whether you truly need them. My guess is not, after so many months of not being used. They can be donated. The exception here are large serving dishes or roasting pans that only get used for holidays or large family gatherings. Although you need these if you're hosting those gatherings, you could consider keeping them outside of the kitchen in a pantry or on a basement shelf, for example, if your kitchen is short on space.

☐ Once you've emptied everything out and decided what stays and what goes, clean the cabinets well. Use a vacuum and/or wipes. A Magic Eraser will help to remove any stubborn scuff marks.

☐ If you need any cupboard organizers, measure well, make a list, and go get them.

☐ Then place like items together in the cabinets in a way that makes sense for how you work in your kitchen. For example, pots and pans should be near the stove, and mugs should be near the coffee maker.

> **A decluttered home matters because**
>
> "I don't want to feel reluctance at inviting guests inside because of my unorganized home."

Look at you go! Your kitchen is almost finished!

☐ Day 9 complete

Day 10—Clear Off the Counters

The final step in decluttering your kitchen in the 10-Day Decluttering Shortcut is to clear off the counters.

Kitchen counters needn't be an eyesore, and they aren't meant to be a landing place for everything. They should provide a place to prepare food and meals. And aside from a few necessary or pretty things, they should remain fairly empty between uses.

To clear off the counters:

☐ Mentally divide your kitchen into zones—cooking, prep, dishwashing, coffee, etc. If it helps, you could draw a quick sketch of your zones.

☐ Now take a look at the counters and what's currently on them. Throw away any trash or loose papers that didn't get tackled on a previous day of the challenge.

☐ Start on one side of the kitchen and work your way around the room, asking yourself if each item really belongs there or if it could be put away in a cabinet or drawer. Put away anything that can be put away. And then make sure whatever remains is in a good location that makes sense for its use. Because our kids are older and everyone has different schedules, we have several people using items in our kitchen, and everything that is out on the counter literally gets daily use. So, our counters are a little fuller than I'd like. But the toaster, microwave, kettle, blender, coffee maker, mugs, and cutting board are all necessary to three meals a day being made here. I do, however, keep the island mostly clear of clutter. The only things that live on the island counters are the dish soap, hand soap, and counter spray all corralled on a pretty cake stand or tray and the dish drying mats (which are neutral-colored, low profile, and blend in well). I may have a vase of flowers and a candle out sometimes too. But at nine feet long, our island can handle that without looking cluttered.

☐ Once you've cleared the counters of items that don't belong and reorganized them so they make sense, give them a thorough wipe down.

Pro Tip: One way to help kitchen counters remain clutter-free is to corral items onto trays as I mentioned with the hand soap, dish soap, and counter spray. We do this with coffee things like syrups as well as with spices in our kitchen.

Yippee! Your kitchen and entryway are now both clutter-free!

☐ Day 10 complete

Okay, now that you've tackled your entire entry and a few high-clutter parts of the kitchen, let's do one big sweep of the house for items that can be gotten rid of without any big effort on your part to add to your small wins that feel like big accomplishments.

CHAPTER 2

120 Things to Throw Away—Guilt-Free

Sometimes it can be hard to figure out which things to get rid of when our house feels overrun with clutter. There are sentimental items and family hand-me-downs that can cause guilt and other strong feelings when we try to declutter them, and that can make the decluttering process extra difficult. We will get to those things later. For now, though, we're going to continue our small wins strategy and get more things cleaned out quickly. To help you do this and build confidence in your decluttering abilities at the same time, I'm sharing a big list of one hundred and twenty things that you can check off as you toss 'em! But first, let's quickly look at what to do with the things you're purging from your home.

What to Do with Your Discarded Items

When I say "things to throw away," it's just a blanket statement. I don't necessarily mean that you'll throw them in the trash. We are charged with the task of taking care of this earth by our heavenly Father, and take care of it we must. There are many options for what you can do with your stuff when it no longer serves you. When you're decluttering and getting rid of stuff, think about where it will end up and what that will do to our planet. Even if you're feeling overwhelmed by your decluttering, try to part with your items in the most environmentally friendly way possible. Below is a list of ideas for what to do with the items you no longer want. Start at the top of the list below (the least wasteful) and move down (the most wasteful) as you purge items.

1. Return any items that are new, with tags, or are otherwise unused. Get a refund or even just store credit to use at a later date when you actually need something.

2. Give to friends/family who love your style or who are in need in this season. Bless them with your abundance.

3. Repurpose things in a way you hadn't necessarily thought of before. Maybe you have one too many baskets, but you need a new end table. Flip that basket upside down and add a top made of a wood round. There are plenty of ideas for repurposing things online if you look. *But use this with caution* and don't use it as an excuse to hold on to too many things for too long, especially if they're broken. "If you've had something for more than six months, and it's still not repaired, it's clutter."[1]

4. Donate to local charities, churches, or shelters that may need the things you're parting with. Old furniture, clothes, books, and kitchen wares can be of great use to some of these places:

- American or Canadian Red Cross
- Buy Nothing Groups on Facebook
- Diabetes Canada
- Dress for Success
- Free the Girls
- Freecycle
- Goodwill

- Habitat for Humanity
- Habitat for Humanity ReStore
- Local shelters like the YMCA or pregnancy help centers
- Planet Aid
- Teen Challenge
- The Salvation Army
- Value Village

5. Sell your items to a variety of places. Sometimes selling your purged items is worth it; sometimes it's just not. If you have any high-value items in great shape, then you could consider selling them. If your items are priced right, someone will likely snap them up in a hurry.

But more often than not, in my personal experience, the time and mental space it takes to prepare something for sale, decide on a price, list it online (or my least favorite, organize a garage sale), negotiate price, and then get it to the person is just not worth it. I'd much rather donate it to a local thrift store or nonprofit in my area.

If you need the money from selling your purged item, however, and you have the time, I highly recommend setting up a holding space for only those items somewhere in your home while you declutter. That way you can simply move sellable items there as you declutter and deal with them all at once when you are finished with the decluttering process. In this way you're saving time by batching tasks. Then sell them at places such as these:

- Craigslist
- Decluttr
- eBay
- Etsy
- Facebook Marketplace
- Garage sale
- Half Price Books stores
- H&M ReWear
- Instagram
- Kijiji
- Local consignment stores
- Mercari
- Poshmark
- Swappa
- thredUP
- Yard sale

6. Recycle your items in typical municipal recycling programs or at specialty recycling centers and programs like the following:

- Nike—Check your local Nike to see if they're accepting running shoes to recycle into their Nike Grind material.
- H&M Garment Collecting program—Hand in any clothes (not just those from H&M) and get a "thank you" voucher to use toward your next purchase. Once you've dropped off your previously loved fashion, H&M's partner I:CO takes over. They empty the boxes and sort the contents into three categories:

  Rewear: Wearable clothes are marketed as second-hand clothing.

  Reuse: If the clothes or textiles are not suitable for rewear, they're turned into other products, such as remake collections or cleaning cloths.

  Recycle: All other clothes and textiles are shredded into textile fibers and used to make, for example, insulation materials.
- Madewell Forever—Get $20 off a new pair of jeans for every pair you drop off at the store. Pairs that have seen better days get recycled into housing insulation through Cotton's Blue Jeans Go Green™ program.
- Stores like Apple, Staples, and Best Buy also have electronics recycling programs, which is a great option whether your municipality has electronics recycling or not.

7. Trash your beyond-donable and beyond-fixable items that can't be recycled in your local landfill. But only do this as a last resort. Under no circumstances should you just toss the items because you're feeling lazy. As Christians and plain old humans who need the earth to thrive, we need to take care of it the best we possibly can. It's just good stewardship.

Some of the ideas listed in this chapter for selling, donating, and recycling items and their locations and programs may have changed between when I was writing this and when it's published. If you want to check on any of them or find other options, just do an online search for "used clothing/tech/household donations" or "recycling programs for used home goods/clothing/tech."

120 Things to Get Rid Of

Think about this for a second before you begin. If clutter causes stress, which we know it does, how much *less* stress will you feel by removing 120 useless items from your home? Like you can finally take a full deep breath, or a weight has been lifted off your shoulders? Like you were actually creating a peaceful dwelling place and an undisturbed place of rest in your home?

Below you will find a list of 120 things that you can part with (*appropriately* trash, donate, or recycle) guilt-free because they are not serving a purpose in *your* home anymore and they're adding stress to your life.

> **A decluttered home matters because**
>
> "It gives me peace and allows me to feel like I can relax and allow myself time to do other things I enjoy."

Don't get caught in the weeds as you go through this list. Avoid getting distracted by other things, or sentimental items, and just move through the list quickly. We will learn how to deal with the tough stuff and tackle each and every room in depth soon.

Got it? Clear?

Okay, here goes the list . . .

- ☐ Worn out shoes (You can recycle runners at Nike stores to have them turned into Nike Grind material that gets reused to make new shoes.)
- ☐ Uncomfortable shoes you never wear
- ☐ Holey rain boots
- ☐ Broken umbrellas
- ☐ Old clothes or clothes you haven't worn in the last year (Unless you are or have been pregnant during that time. In which case, you get a pass on this for another year.)

☐ Old formal wear—bridesmaid's dresses, prom dresses, tuxes, and all the accessories that go with them

☐ Free advertising hats or T-shirts—like that one you got when you signed up for a credit card at the ball game (Wait, was that just Dean and me? M'kay. Moving on then.)

☐ Old or damaged purses, bags, or luggage

☐ Socks without mates

☐ Irreparable holey socks

☐ Too-small kids' clothing that doesn't hold any special memories (Remember, we'll deal with sentimental items in chapter 6.)

☐ Wire or plastic hangers from the store (Use matching hangers in your closets at home for a more organized and streamlined look and feel.)

☐ Hangers from the dry cleaners (You may be able to return these for the cleaners to reuse. It doesn't hurt to ask. Worst case, they say no, and you recycle the hangers instead.)

☐ Extra buttons—you know, the ones they attach in a little baggie, just in case, that you *never* use

☐ Tarnished or broken jewelry and earrings without a match

☐ Broken or damaged hair ties and clips

☐ Old glasses (You can donate them to most optometrists, who will then get them to people in need.)

☐ Old makeup

☐ Beauty products that you tried and didn't like (You may be able to return them or donate them to local homeless shelters and women's shelters.)

☐ Old or more toxic skincare if you've switched to more natural products

☐ Beauty and makeup samples (I adore Sephora, but man, do I ever loathe all the extra clutter caused by so many samples!)

☐ Dried-out nail polish and worn nail files

☐ Used loofahs and poufs in the shower (If they can't be washed in hot water, they're likely full of germs.)

☐ Everyone's toothbrush (Toothbrushes should be changed every three months, or after any illness. If it's been a while, toss 'em. (Just make sure you have a replacement first!)

☐ Hotel toiletries—unless you use them regularly or have plans to within the next two months

☐ Soap scraps and empty soap bottles

☐ Expired medicine/vitamins (Check the FDA's website in the US or its counterpart in your country for details on how to safely dispose of old medicines.)

☐ Expired sunscreen and bug sprays

☐ Old chargers and cables

☐ Old tech devices—VHS player, cassette player, etc., if you don't use them

☐ Mixed tapes and old CDs (Only keep the ones you regularly listen to.)

☐ Movies you don't love (We still keep some Blu-rays/DVDs, but *only* of movies we love and rewatch repeatedly.)

☐ CD and DVD stands and storage pieces after you've gotten rid of the CDs and DVDs

☐ Old remotes

☐ Old video games

☐ Old cell phones and their gear

☐ Dead batteries (Be sure to check your area's battery recycling options specifically for rechargeable batteries.)

☐ Burned-out light bulbs

☐ Flash drives (Be sure to transfer anything useful to the cloud first.)

☐ Extra or broken headphones or earbuds

☐ Excess phone cases—especially if they don't fit your current phone

☐ Duplicate computer accessories—mice, keyboards, etc.

☐ Product boxes (Keep them for up to three months in case you'll have to make a return, then get rid of them. Exceptions would be expensive tech devices that you may want to later resell with the box, such as a smartphone or game system.)

☐ Manuals for products you don't have anymore

☐ Manuals that can be found online

☐ Take-out menus

☐ Extra or old calendars

☐ Old newspapers and magazines

☐ Business cards (There's the internet and LinkedIn for that these days!)

☐ Expired coupons

☐ Expired insurance papers for your home and cars

☐ Rewards cards or old bank or credit cards (Make sure they're well destroyed before tossing them so they can't be used in identity theft.)

☐ Receipts not needed for tax purposes, warranties, or returns

☐ Unused or filled notebooks and binders

☐ Filled up, used up, and finished coloring/puzzle books

☐ Used up/dried out pens, highlighters, and markers

☐ Cards and invitations—either file them away in a keepsake binder or box or get rid of them altogether. (Again, we'll talk more about memorabilia later.)

☐ Books that you aren't reading or that are literally falling apart in your hands

☐ Toys your kids don't play with anymore

☐ Broken toys

☐ Old Halloween costumes

☐ Completed school projects that have already been graded

☐ Old backpacks that no longer fit or are broken beyond repair

☐ Old board games—especially if they're missing pieces

☐ Pet toys that your pet doesn't play with, or that are broken or very chewed up

- ☐ Old pet clothes/collars that don't fit your pet anymore, or ones that are broken or very worn
- ☐ Expired pet medications (Some vet offices are happy to take back many medicines that your pet no longer needs, especially flea/tick and heartworm medicine.)
- ☐ Expired food (Don't forget to check your freezer along with your fridge and pantry. No food stays good forever!)
- ☐ Moldy or otherwise gross leftovers
- ☐ Food boxes (Decant things like cereal into pretty jars or more suitable sealed containers.)
- ☐ Unidentified frozen objects in your freezer
- ☐ Old spices (Most should be used up or tossed within twelve months; if they don't have a scent, their flavor is gone.)
- ☐ Takeout condiments (How many Chick-fil-A sauces do you really need? For real?)
- ☐ Plastic utensils from takeout
- ☐ Old cookware/bakeware that you haven't used for months
- ☐ Random bottles and jars you've been keeping just in case—for way too long
- ☐ Single-function small appliances like bread makers (If you never use them, what's the point of them taking up space in your kitchen and brain?)
- ☐ Stained or warped plastic storage containers (That spaghetti sauce is not coming out, sweetie!)
- ☐ Used vegetable oil from frying foods
- ☐ Duplicate or broken kitchen tools that are still kicking around
- ☐ Excess mugs (Most of us could stand to get rid of at least a few!)
- ☐ Chipped or broken dishware, mugs, and glasses
- ☐ Random drinking glasses
- ☐ Rusted utensils like steak knives
- ☐ Rusted baking pans, cookie sheets, and muffin tins

- ☐ Stained tea towels, dishcloths, napkins, and tablecloths you just can't get clean
- ☐ Old water bottles and travel mugs that leak
- ☐ Outgrown kids plastic dish sets (The exception would be if they're still used for guests, but then only keep what you really need.)
- ☐ Your dish sponge or scrubby (If it's more than a month old, it's probably full of gross germs.)
- ☐ Cookbooks you never use (Most recipes can be found online these days, so only keep the cookbooks that you refer to again and again.)
- ☐ Cleaning rags (You really only need a few since you can wash them.)
- ☐ Worn-out towels (If you don't have enough cleaning rags, you can cut one towel up into rags, but get rid of the rest.)
- ☐ Old or extra towels and bedding that you hate or that don't get used
- ☐ Old lumpy pillows
- ☐ Foam throw pillow inserts (Switch to down or down alternative for way nicer pillows that will hold their shape and last much longer.)
- ☐ Old curtains that don't fit your current windows
- ☐ Decor that doesn't match your style anymore (If you don't know what your style is or why it matters, check out my course Decorating Uncomplicated at HomeMadeLovely.com /Decorating-Uncomplicated.)
- ☐ Broken picture frames (Perhaps it's time to upgrade?)
- ☐ Stale potpourri
- ☐ Burned-down, useless stumps of candles
- ☐ Old paint (Well-sealed paint can be kept for years at an even temperature, but most of us don't seal it well enough or we keep it in the garage or shed where it's exposed to a range of temperatures. Be sure to dispose of these correctly.)

☐ Extra flowerpots

☐ Extra holiday décor (A good rule of thumb is if you haven't put it out in two years, it's time for it to go!)

☐ Unraveled gift bows.

☐ Wrapping-paper scraps. (If the amount of paper is too small to wrap most gifts, get rid of it!)

☐ Half-finished craft projects

☐ Craft supply scraps

☐ Supplies for hobbies you no longer pursue

☐ Dirty air filters (Check them once a month and make sure you're changing them as soon as they start to look dirty.)

☐ Old, used motor oil

☐ Random nails, nuts, bolts, and screws

☐ Extra screws, nails, and Allen keys that came with your purchases

☐ Scrap wood (If you don't have a specific project in mind for it, get rid of it!)

☐ Random key chains

☐ Unidentifiable keys, or keys to old places or vehicles

☐ Old license plates for cars you're not driving (Check if you're supposed to return them to your licensing office or DMV.)

☐ Instruments no one has played in years—donate them so someone can use them.

☐ Instrument gear for instruments you no longer have

☐ Old sports equipment that isn't being used

☐ Exercise equipment that hasn't been used for a year or more

☐ Exercise clothes that don't fit or that are worn through

Look at you go!

Okay, so now that you've made some progress on the easier-to-part-with clutter, let's work on that mind of yours.

PART 2

BUILD A DECLUTTERING MINDSET

CHAPTER 3

Four Reasons to Simplify Your Home

There are many authors and bloggers who promote a minimalist lifestyle, for obvious reasons—it's simple and it's clutter-free. Other minimalists like Myquillyn Smith (aka The Nester) and Allie Casazza have adapted minimalism to suit their lives and share it from a nontraditional perspective. Even with that loosening of the minimalist rules, I'm personally still not a minimalist. At least not yet. I like my stuff. But I do believe that it stands to reason that the more stuff you have, the more *work* you will have to do to keep track and take care of it all. Another way to look at it is that whatever you have in your home is like *inventory* that you have to manage. The more things you have, the more things you have to maintain, clean, and take care of. The more *work* you have to do. So, the more you reasonably simplify—keeping just the right things for the way you want to live your life—the less work you will have to do.

Regardless of how you want your home to feel, or how you live your life, living with *too much stuff* is time-consuming and takes up mental space in your brain. "Clutter has become a cultural obsession—we're drowning in stuff."[1] And clutter "gets in our way, both physically and mentally. It impacts our ability to focus, and it undermines our productivity."[2]

So even though I don't subscribe to minimalism per se, I do think we could all do with a little less stuff. Need more convincing? Here are four major reasons to simplify your home:

1. You Will Enjoy Less Visual Clutter

I like our house to be cozy. But I don't like it to be overrun with stuff. Because I change up our decor with the seasons, in the past it's been really easy for me to go overboard and fill it with too much. But when the house starts to get too full, I can feel it. Like it's all creeping in and suffocating me. Plus, we have five grown people and a dog living here, which equals plenty of stuff. It's no fun tripping over things on the stairs just waiting to be put away. I dislike looking at fifty pairs of shoes in the entryway. Okay, maybe it's only ten pairs of shoes, but it's still too many. I don't want to see now-too-small sweaters in a pile on the kids' bedroom floors. I need some walls to have nothing on them. For real. I've learned that it's so much more soothing to look around and not have every corner piled and covered with stuff. It's so much nicer to have some white space. If you simplify and declutter, you will allow your house to *visually* breathe. And that will help you to *literally* breathe a little easier too.

> "Clutter is not just the stuff on your floor—it's anything that stands between you and the life you want to be living."
>
> —PETER WALSH

2. You'll Have Less to Clean

Seriously, who likes cleaning? If you do, come to my house every Friday and I'll pay you with coffee in exchange for your cleaning services. With less stuff in the house, there's less to clean, vacuum around, and dust. Keep this in mind as you declutter—only keep the things you love so much that cleaning them and taking care of them is worth the joy they bring you. Having less stuff to clean makes it 100% worth it to simplify and declutter your home, in my opinion.

3. You'll Spend Less Time Organizing

It's awesome to be organized! Organizing our space is one of my favorite things to do. I know, I'm a weirdo and a totally traditional organizer. But I only love to organize the things that we actually need or love. Like spices in the pantry or towels in the closet. It's pretty pointless and quite frustrating to organize the stuff that's unnecessary. The goal isn't just to move all the stuff around. *Decluttering cannot just be replaced with more organizing.* Let that sink in. *Attempting to organize clutter is an exercise in futility.* It's a complete waste of time and energy. Instead, get rid of what you don't need, and I promise getting and keeping what's left organized will be so much easier.

4. You Can Help Others

Here's something else to keep in mind: While you may not need that thingamabob or doohickey taking up space in the corner, *someone else may be looking for that very thing.* Maybe someone needs decor for their first apartment, and you've just redecorated and have several pretty things that just don't work in your home anymore. Or perhaps you now work from home and don't need that perfectly lovely business suit. Or maybe that new mom down the street could really use those baby things that you're finished with. You can be an absolute blessing to someone else, just by passing along what you no longer need. When you simplify, consider donating your unneeded items that are in good shape to local and national nonprofits, your church, or friends. You may never know how much help it will be!

CHAPTER 4

The Clutter Personalities

Okay, so now that you know from a bird's-eye view why it's beneficial to get rid of clutter, let's talk about how we accumulate it in the first place, aka the Clutter Personalities.

Much like we don't gain those extra ten or twenty pounds overnight, clutter takes time to pile up. Yet at the same time, it seems to sneak up on us, doesn't it? You know what I mean, right? One day your jeans fit, then the next week they're a wee bit tighter, and then a couple of weeks later you can't button them up anymore. Many of us end up with a houseful of clutter the same way we gain weight—little by little and entirely unintentionally. (If you're blessed to be naturally thin, just go with me here, okay?)

So, why do we accumulate all that clutter? Much as it's hard to fight an enemy we can't see or identify, if we don't know why we have the clutter, it's going to be difficult to stop its accumulation. "Both inside your home and inside your head can get cluttered all too easily, and if we can't identify the issue and deal with that, then **the clutter will keep coming back** no matter how much decluttering we do—decluttering is only the surface layer—you have to **understand the underlying issues** to make it a permanent change."[1]

To help you understand your clutter and how to stop it, below are ten reasons, which I refer to as Clutter Personalities, why we collect clutter and how to stop each one in its tracks. As you go through these, take note of which one most describes you and the clutter in your home. You may fall into several of the categories, but one will likely feel more like you than the rest.

1. You Are a Worrywart

The Worrywart collects clutter by *excessively* stocking up or holding on to things "just in case" they are needed someday. Stocking up or holding on to *everything* in this way isn't helpful and is stressing you out for no good reason. Some of these tendencies likely developed in your family of origin, as in your parents and/or grandparents likely accumulated the same kind of clutter. Many Worrywarts accept more than needed hand-me-downs from friends and family. Maybe it's not clothing like it was when we were kids, but instead, it's furniture, or dishes, or tools, or whatever. There's absolutely nothing wrong with hand-me-downs at all! We've given and received some awesome hand-me-downs, and they can be a lifesaver in a financially tight season of life. But if your house is full of clutter because you've accepted every hand-me-down ever offered to you, even if you didn't need it, then that's a problem. A problem that is likely due to fear and a scarcity mindset in which you worry that you may not have enough of that thing later, so you'd better accept it now. My friend, you need to work on that issue. Because I guarantee it's affecting more than just the clutter in your home.

Of course, historic and recent events like pandemics and natural disasters have shown us that it's a good idea to have a *reasonable* number of consumables such as toilet paper, shelf-stable or frozen foods, and disinfectants on hand at any given time. But there's a difference between being prepared and hoarding. There's no need to stock up excessively on those things or on things you wouldn't actually ever use (like ten pounds of lasagna when you're allergic to wheat) or that you wouldn't use in a few months' time. And in most cases, you really don't need to have an extra vegetable peeler or hammer filling up your kitchen drawers or garage "just in case." Most of us live near enough a hardware store, convenience store, or big-box store that we can get things like that when they're needed. And friends are often happy to lend a hand if buying something new is not possible right away. So, don't collect anything *just in case*. It's unnecessary and can cause *much* clutter in your home.

How to conquer this type of clutter collecting

If you are a Worrywart and are afraid you won't have something when you need it later, work on your mindset. Chapter 8 will be immensely helpful to you—for *all* the clutter and all the worry in your life. Refocus, take inventory of what you have, and recognize that you have what you need *right now*. Put Post-it notes on your mirror that say, "I have what I need for today." Get counseling or prayer or find a good book on improving your mindset. Practice affirmations daily that say you have what you need when you need it. (More on affirmations in chapter 8.) And know with a deep knowing that your Father God has got you and that He will look after your needs when they arise. Matthew 6:25–34 reminds us of this godly provision:

"Therefore I tell you, do not worry about your life, what you will eat or drink; or about your body, what you will wear. Is not life more than food, and the body more than clothes? Look at the birds of the air; they do not sow or reap or store away in barns, and yet your heavenly Father feeds them. Are you not much more valuable than they? Can any one of you by worrying add a single hour to your life?

"And why do you worry about clothes? See how the flowers of the field grow. They do not labor or spin. Yet I tell you that not even Solomon in all his splendor was dressed like one of these. If that is how God clothes the grass of the field, which is here today and tomorrow is thrown into the fire, will he not much more clothe you—you of little faith? So do not worry, saying, 'What shall we eat?' or 'What shall we drink?' or 'What shall we wear?' For the pagans run after all these things, and your heavenly Father knows that you need them. But seek first his kingdom and his righteousness, and all these things will be given to you as well. Therefore do not worry about tomorrow, for tomorrow will worry about itself."

In addition to working on your mindset and releasing the fears associated with not having enough, you need to stop accepting every hand-me-down that is offered to you. A polite "no thank you—but keep me in mind in the future" will go a long way. Going forward, only graciously accept the gift of hand-me-downs *if* you genuinely need them right now, or you know you will need them shortly (like for the impending birth of a baby), or if it is better quality or fit than something you already have (then you need to get rid of the old something immediately, so you're not accumulating more clutter).

A decluttered home matters because

"Clutter makes me anxious. So, clutter-free is relaxing."

Remember, whatever you have in your home is like inventory that you have to manage and maintain. You don't want to do extra *unnecessary* work. And God does not want us to live in fear. He wants us to live abundant lives filled with grace and gratitude.

2. You Are a Delayer

The Delayer says, "I'll get to it later." It is said that the best time to plant a tree was twenty years ago and the second-best time is now. I believe the same idea applies to decluttering your home. It's better not to let the clutter in at all. But if you have, now is the time to get it out! My friend, you will need to tackle your clutter at some point in order to free yourself from your stuff. And living in a cleaner, tidier, calmer home is definitely worth the work now.

How to conquer this type of clutter collecting

There are a few reasons why Delayers put off decluttering until someday in the future.

If you just don't feel like doing it, consider this your gentle kick in the rear to get it done already. You need to just start! It's easier to keep a rolling stone in motion once it's going. Work on getting motivated by focusing on the end-result feelings versus the ones you're feeling now. Your clutter is not serving you; it's weighing you down. Set a timer and follow the steps in this book! Don't use excuses to procrastinate.

If you've looked at some of your clutter and thought you'd turn it into something cool *one day* or list it on eBay *some other day,* just do yourself a favor and throw it out or donate it *now. A good guideline is if you've held on to something and thought about repurposing or fixing it for six months and haven't done anything with it, it's time to part with it.*

And finally, if your "I'll get to it later" clutter is made up of sentimental things, my advice for clearing it out is the same as many other people's—tackle the *nonsentimental* stuff first. Use the quick wins tools I gave you in part 1. Once you have some "getting rid of" under your belt, you'll feel more inspired and capable of decluttering the tough stuff. You'll have more confidence in your ability to sort and discard. I'll talk more about how to handle sentimental clutter in chapter 6. For now, it's good enough to know that this is a very common type of clutter for people, but it still needs to be dealt with.

3. You Are a Bargain Hunter

Bargain Hunters are treasure seekers who tend to look for worth or value in things. They're always searching for a feel-better fix by buying new things to fill an emptiness inside—a new purse, new shoes, more decor. But you know that's not where the real treasure of life lies.

This type of clutter is also sometimes accumulated because of the thrill of finding a bargain and the feeling that we're getting a deal. I mean really, is there a better feeling than finding your favorite name-brand pair of jeans that fit you *perfectly,* for 75% off? Or getting four snow tires for the price of two when it's time to switch over for winter (talk about #adulting)? Or stumbling upon a two-liter bottle of your favorite shampoo at the mall for the same price as the tiny bottle you usually buy at your salon? Such a great feeling, right? I love that feeling. But that bargain-hunting thrill can get us into trouble if we buy things *only* because they are a deal and *not* because we actually need them. Let me clarify. If you need a new pair of jeans, by all means, buy the pair that's on sale for 75% off. The same goes for the winter tires and the shampoo. *But* if you already have ten pairs of perfectly fitting jeans, you don't need another pair. And if you have brand-new snow tires in the garage from the end-of-season sale last year, there's no reason to buy the two-for-one deal right now. And if you have a pixie cut like I used to, it's going to take you a loonnnggg time to use up two liters of shampoo. This means if you succumb to those deals and buy things when you don't need them, you will find that your drawers, cabinets, and garage are stuffed much fuller than you'd like them to be.

Bargain Hunters also tend to overestimate the value of their things, and letting go of things you paid good money for can seem wasteful. But once you accept that the money is already gone, it's much easier to part with the items you don't actually need.

How to conquer this type of clutter collecting

Counteract this type of clutter by thinking logically about your needs and your available space when you're shopping. Stay off social media if seeing other people's stuff makes you want more. Try a no-spend month to help you break the habit of shopping unnecessarily. Get professional help if your shopping is an addiction, or join a group like Shopaholics Anonymous. And never again buy anything *just* because it's on sale.

4. You Are a Wishful Thinker

Ah, the aspirational, wishful thinking type of clutter. It's another one of those seemingly well-meaning types of clutter, like accepting too many hand-me-downs or holding on to too many heirlooms. What is the Wishful Thinker, you ask? Well, some of us have clutter in our home that is the result of things we've collected because we "wannabe" or dream of being something. Like that summer you wanted to take up hot yoga to help you reduce stress, but you gave up after a few tries because all that "ohm-ing" and contorting your poor body in the extreme heat made you feel more stressed instead of less. Or when you thought it would be fun to host Fondue Fridays every week with your friends and then figured out half of them don't eat dairy. And there you are now with all the yoga mats and blocks and fondue pots and sticks just collecting dust shoved in a corner somewhere.

How to conquer this type of clutter collecting

Listen, we all aspire to try new things and be better people. It's a good thing to better yourself, and trying new things is one of the joys of this life on earth. But if you have tried something and decided it's just not for you or you'd rather not do it again, and you haven't used the things that go with that aspiration in a while, it's time to clear them out of your home. Maybe by doing that you will even help someone else who will really love yoga or who has dairy-loving friends! Plus, you'll reduce your clutter—and your stress—no yoga required!

(I have nothing against yoga or fondue, by the way. If you love them, awesome! Those were just examples. Other examples include all manner of discarded hobby supplies like knitting needles and yarn, weights and gym equipment, art supplies, camping equipment, model trains, canning jars, cake-making pans and icing tips, embroidery hoops and floss, jewelry making tools, tennis balls and racquets, snorkeling gear, gardening tools . . . the list could go on and on. If you tried it and don't want to do it again, get rid of the stuff!)

5. You Are an Idealist

The Idealist has too much clutter because she thinks, *Next week I'll do it perfectly*—which is different from the Delayer, who just keeps putting off an unpleasant task. This desire for perfectionism keeps the Idealist from taking any action at all. But I've got news for you, lovely: *perfect is impossible*. It's not gonna happen. You're going to have to do some decluttering and then do some more. You will make a mess before it gets better. And it will never be 100% perfect. But it will be *better*.

How to conquer this type of clutter collecting

Repeat after me: "Done is better than perfect." Practice the affirmations in chapter 8. Choose a method of decluttering from chapter 11 that fits your current season of life and *just get started*. You do *not* have to do this perfectly. You *do* have to make progress.

And hey, if you're really stubborn and stuck on decluttering perfectly, there's always the saying that "practice makes perfect." And you can't get to "perfect" without practicing—aka taking action. ;) So, just get started already!

6. You Are a Hurrier

The Hurrier is someone whose clutter has accumulated because you have too much going on and you're constantly running around frazzled. This leads to buying duplicates of items you already own because you don't have organized spaces and you have to search a million places to find what you need. So, you quit searching and just buy another version of the thing. Later, you'll likely find the original somewhere random in your house, by which time, it's too late—the clutter has begun, and you've wasted time and money. Just look at these stats: "Americans [spend] 2.5 days a year looking for misplaced items. . . . We collectively spend $2.7 billion each year replacing items, and more than half of us are regularly late for work or school due to frustrating searches."[2] Who wants to feel frazzled and have to waste money to buy things they own but can't find? And who loves the feeling of rushing and showing up late because they can't find the keys? Declutter so you don't have to suffer like this anymore!

How to conquer this type of clutter collecting

If you find that you are too busy and rushed to declutter your home, slow down and prioritize what actually needs doing. Then make an appointment with yourself and put decluttering in your schedule just like you would any important appointment. Because it is important! Keep that appointment with yourself; make it nonnegotiable like the dentist or optometrist. Fit in your decluttering either in several smaller sprint-style bursts or in one or two longer marathons (more on the three decluttering methods in chapter 11). Because if you don't plan to make time to declutter, you'll find yourself running late while you look for the things you can't find in your mess!

7. You Are a Statue

Sometimes we just get so worn out and busy with life that we inadvertently hold on to all the things because we have no idea where to start—and then by the time we finally come up for air and notice the mess, we try very hard to ignore it because we feel so overwhelmed. I get it. When we are overwhelmed, we don't know where to begin and we feel *paralyzed*. It's okay, lovely. Sometimes life just gets whacko, and there are seasons in life that are much more intense than others. Bringing a new baby home, for example. Or caring for aging parents. Or a pandemic and stay-at-home orders. Those are hard seasons, and you should give yourself some extra grace and leniency during them. But you do need to take the time as soon as possible to clear out any clutter and then set up systems that will help you keep it out in the future. Once your systems are in place, habits (which I will help you with in chapter 14) are going to be your best friend in avoiding that overwhelmed feeling again, *even when life throws you another curveball.*

How to conquer this type of clutter collecting

Begin by identifying specifically what the clutter is—trash, new purchases, party decorations, seasonal décor, gifts—and determine to stop accumulating it. *If you are overwhelmed, don't try to declutter your entire house in a weekend.* That is not going to help you at all. Instead, tackle one small space at a time or try one of the other two decluttering methods from chapter 11. This will help you reduce your clutter, and it will give you the confidence to tackle larger and larger spaces until your whole house is finally clutter-free. And then really pay attention to chapter 14 for setting up your rhythms and routines to become habits that you can more easily follow during the next onset of hard life events.

8. You Are a Memory Keeper

If you're collecting clutter associated with memories, you're holding on to things because of their *perceived* emotional hold over you or their perceived value. When you look at these things, you think of the person who gave them to you, and that brings back a flood of memories. Or you don't want to hurt their feelings by getting rid of the items they've given you or passed down to you. It's okay to feel this way. But when you can't part with *anything* because of this, that's a big problem.

How to conquer this type of clutter collecting

If you collect sentimental clutter, you need to work on separating people and emotions from things. Start with easy items when decluttering. Then, save only the most important things that bring you the most joy. And definitely study chapter 6 for how to deal with sentimental clutter in detail.

9. You Are a Giftee

Gift clutter can be a little trickier to wade through because this kind of clutter piles up from the best of intentions (much like the wishful thinking or aspirational type of clutter). You have people who love you and want to bless you with things. Maybe people whose love language is gifts. And you don't want to hurt anyone's feelings. I really don't either. In fact, I tend to avoid confrontation at all costs. Getting rid of gifts that people have given you tends to stir up feelings of guilt and thoughts like *How could I get rid of this lamp that my great aunt bought me?* But remember, their gift was meant to bless you, not burden you. *Honesty*—in a kind way, of course—is

> **A decluttered home matters because**
>
> "It brings a sense of balance and peace."

really the best policy. I mean, if people are giving you gifts that are not useful or wanted, it's not just cluttering up your house . . . it's wasting their money too. Even if they don't see it that way at first.

How to conquer this type of clutter collecting

Sit down and have conversations with family and friends about what you do and don't like or want to have in your home. Speak up and ask for the types of gifts you would genuinely appreciate. Or choose to make memories and have experiences instead of getting things you don't need. Or ask for perishable things like food or flowers that won't take up space permanently in your home but will bring joy to both you and the gift-giver. If your family and friends want to continue to gift you things that you don't need for birthdays, anniversaries, holidays, and the like, graciously accept and then pass them along to someone who could use them later. Just because the giver gives a gift does not mean you have to keep it forever. And take the initiative and ask your friends and family about their preferences too. They may appreciate your thoughtfulness! We'll talk more about getting your family on board in chapter 7.

10. You Are a Creative

You love to create—food, art, crafts, you name it. But cleaning up isn't very creative, so you leave a mess in your wake. Knitting needles protrude from the couch cushions, the sink is always full of mixing bowls and spoons, and your paint cans are taking up half the hallway. We have one of these in our house. There is always a mess in her beautifully creative wake. That right-braininess is an incredible gift, but if you're a Creative, you need to balance it out a little if you want to have the peace and calm that comes with living a more clutter-free life.

How to conquer this type of clutter collecting

Creatives tend to have a hard time with organization and structure. They don't work well with traditional organization because it's too much work; plus their minds are either already onto the next thing before they finish what they're currently working on, or they're so engrossed in their current project that nothing else seems to matter. *But knowing this is the key.* Once you do, you can set up systems and storage that work with your natural tendencies, which will help immensely with your messes. *In the next chapter, we're going to investigate the Organizing Personalities, and big hint: Creatives are generally Everything Out + Simple Organizers!* But first, answer the worksheet questions on the next page to identify the reasons you've collected clutter up until this point so you can stop clutter in its tracks going forward.

Why Do You Collect Clutter?

1. Take a quick walk-through of your house. Write down the things you know are clutter in your home.

2. Now identify where those things came from or when. Why did you bring *xyz* into the house? If you didn't bring it in, how did it get there?

3. Now look at your answers to the last two questions and reread the descriptions of the Clutter Personalities in this chapter. What type of Clutter Personality do you have? Remember, you may identify with more than one, and that's okay. Jot down the names of the two that best describe you.

4. Now jot down a few ideas on how to stop collecting clutter in this way. Review *"How to conquer this type of clutter collecting"* for each of your top two personalities from this chapter if you need help.

Continue reading to find out how to get organized and clear the clutter from every room in your house.

CHAPTER 5

The Organizing
Personalities

Most of us have a desire to belong, to fit in with others, and to find "our people." At the same time, we have a strong desire to be our own unique individuals. I believe we were hardwired this way from the beginning. This is why doing church as a community is something we as Christians crave, while we revel in knowing that we were each created as different parts of the body of Christ. This is also why we find personality tests and online quizzes so intriguing—they classify us as part of a larger group that is similar to us (feeding into our desire for a sense of belonging and being known and seen), while at the same time reminding us that we are not exactly the same as everyone else (speaking to our individualism). I really like to look at personality categorizations as *a way to lead us to a process or way of doing things that better suits our individual personalities, which can result in better outcomes for our efforts.* That's why I'm going to talk a bit about Organizing Personalities.

Before we get to those specifics, though, I also want you to know that if you feel like you're inherently messy, or if you've tried organizing and failed over and over, and you feel as if there's no hope for you, *it's okay*. It's *not* you. ***You are not messy; you just haven't found*** *an organization system that works for you yet.* The way most people teach organization only fits the personalities of a small portion of the population. It took until I was doing research for this book to realize that in the past, although my intentions were good and I did help people to declutter their homes, I wasn't doing them any favors when I inadvertently taught them to set up organizing systems that worked for me and my Organizing Personality, but that just weren't right for them.

It's also important to note that you or your family members may not fit neatly into one of these four Organizing Personalities. We are, after all, complex individuals with different internal makeups and different backgrounds. You may even lean toward one personality type for your kitchen but prefer a completely different style of organization in your living room, for example. Regardless, as you read on, one Organizing Personality will likely stand out and feel more like you than another, so feel free to use the suggestions for that personality type as best you can.

The Four Organizing Characteristics

In order to describe the four Organizing Personalities, we need to first look at the four different characteristics that they are comprised of. The first two characteristics speak to how we like to see our organization (all out in the open or hidden away) and the second two to how detail-oriented we are (or not) when it comes to organization and actually putting things away when we're done with them. Let's look at those now.

Characteristic 1: Everything Out (EO)

Everything Outs like to have their stuff on display, in plain sight, and out in the open. They appreciate hanging pot racks and knives on a magnetic strip in the kitchen. They love open shelving in a bathroom for towels and toiletries. And they tend to like walk-in closets with open shelving better than dressers with everything hidden out of sight. For the Everything Out person, everything needs to be visible because out of sight means out of mind, which often equals forgotten. They prefer to see everyday items and do best with clearly labeled organization, although they may stuff things frantically in a closet when people are coming over so as not to appear messy. Everything Outs like visual abundance. Everything Outs need simple, out-in-the-open functional storage or they simply won't put things away. Because the bulk of mainstream organization systems hide things away, Everything Out personalities don't do well with them. They have likely tried and failed in the past to get organized, and they think that they are doing something wrong or that they're just messy, when in fact it is the system they're trying to use that is just not right. The Everything Out organizers can benefit from having a friend or family member help with the decision-making and decluttering process by keeping these brilliant multitaskers on track while they declutter and get organized.

Characteristic 2: Nothing Out (NO)

Nothing Outs love to have all their stuff behind closed doors because they hate visual messes. Cabinets and drawers are their very best friends when it comes to organization. Nothing Outs tuck things away out of sight, but without the presence of a good working organizational system that suits them, things get really messy in there because they tend to shove stuff anywhere. Sometimes Nothing Outs will tuck away too much and totally forget what they have. Nothing Outs tend to take pride in an organized and well-decorated home, and they feel in control when things are neat and tidy—even if it just appears that way on the surface. But over time they will feel the mess creeping up on them from behind closed doors and need to tackle even hidden storage spaces to gain some peace with their homes. Nothing Outs like visual simplicity.

Characteristic 3: Simple Organization (SO)

Simple organizers are big-picture thinkers and are not at all detail-oriented. They do much better with large storage containers without lids, if possible, or overall categories of organization—like one folder for all their financial paperwork versus a folder for retirement savings, another for kids' educational savings, and another for their mortgage. Their minds tend to move on to the next thing quickly, and as such, they require fast, easy storage containers that they can just toss their things into when they're tidying up.

Characteristic 4: Detailed Organization (DO)

Detail-oriented people like to put things away in small, specific categories and subcategories—think lots of little containers for office supplies or kitchen gadgets. They are perfectionists and like things done in a certain way. Because of this desire for perfection, they tend to procrastinate on putting things away rather than do it imperfectly, and they can be hard on others who don't get it when it comes to putting things away. They are also often plagued with indecision as they evaluate the best or perfect way to organize things. The good news is that once a good-for-them system is chosen and implemented, and they actually get started, they tend to be really good at keeping things organized and tidy.

> "Holding on to stuff imprisons us; letting go is freeing."
>
> —JOSHUA FIELDS MILLBURN

The Four Organizing Personalities

Okay, now that we've outlined the four characteristics, let's talk about their combinations because those are what make up the four Organizing Personalities.

1. The Everything Out + Simple Organizer (EOSO)

The Everything Out + Simple Organizer can *seem* more cluttered and messier than anyone else, even if they're not, because they don't like to put things away in a detailed or hidden way. They want to see their things, so they don't forget what they have and where it is. Keeping their homes decluttered and on the more minimalistic side will help greatly in the reduction of visual clutter and messes, as will making their organizational systems easy.

Types of organization that work best for Everything Out + Simple Organizers:

- Lots of hooks and pegboards
- Open shelving
- Large drawers and shelves, one per type of thing that needs storing/organizing
- Translucent or transparent storage containers
- Large containers, baskets, and bins *without* lids
- Regular purging sessions to keep the clutter at bay

2. The Everything Out + Detailed Organizer (EODO)

The Everything Out + Detailed Organizer is one of the less common types of organizers. They like to see what they have but also like to keep things organized in smaller categories. Things tend to pile up until they're ready to put them away perfectly. But put away and tidy is better than perfect. Clear organizing containers, labeled and on open shelving, are this personality type's best friend in the whole world.

Types of organization that work for Everything Out + Detailed Organizers:

- Shelving, and lots of it
- Lots of clear bins, jars, and containers, with or without lids
- Labels for every single container and subcategory

3. The Nothing Out + Simple Organizer (NOSO)

The Nothing Out + Simple Organizer loves visual simplicity above all. Their storage needs to be made up of pretty coordinating storage items, like drawer dividers, bins, and baskets, to hide their things out of sight in an organized way. If organization is too complicated, though, the Nothing Out + Simple Organizer will not put things away. Until there is a good system in place, the Nothing Out + Simple Organizer will likely shove things into drawers and cupboards just to get them out of sight.

Types of organization that work best for Nothing Out + Simple Organizers:

- Lots of big drawers for quick tidying up and easy access
- Cabinets and cupboards with doors
- Drawer dividers, but not too many
- Large bins and baskets inside cupboards and closets, with labels
- No lids on storage containers

4. The Nothing Out + Detailed Organizer (NODO)

The Nothing Out + Detailed Organizer is typically very logical and orderly. They *love* to be organized and they revel in the actual process of organizing. This type is the one that all the organizing stores love to sell to. They love detail and all the organizing things. But much like the other organizer types, if a system is not set up, they tend to pile everything. Their piles are very neat and tidy comparatively, but they are piles, nonetheless.

Types of organization that work for Nothing Out + Detailed Organizers:

- Drawers and cupboards with doors
- Multiple drawer organizers and containers in each drawer
- Containers within containers—like a large, lidded tote for sewing supplies, with smaller containers inside for buttons, thread, sewing needles, and scissors
- Labels for every single container and subcategory

	Everything Out	Nothing Out
Simple	EOSO: Prefers to see everything because out of sight equals out of mind, good with visual abundance, big-picture thinkers, not into details.	NOSO: Loves to tuck things away behind closed doors, loves visual simplicity, needs easy-to-use storage solutions, not into details.
Detailed	EODO: Likes to see their things, good with visual abundance but wants things very organized, detail oriented.	NODO: The traditional organizer, likes things hidden away, and loves smaller organization and subcategories of organization.

Different Organizing Personalities under One Roof

Now that you've read through the four Organizing Personalities, you probably understand that we all organize differently. But what do you do when you inevitably have more than one Organizing Personality type living in your home? When one person likes to see things out in the open and another wants things hidden away? Or when someone is really good at sorting things into infinitesimally small categories and someone else just wants to dump things into one big basket? How do you organize your house then? Well, *the general rule for peace and harmony and an organized home is that you always cater to the simplest, most visible storage and organization.* This is because it will be easier for a detailed person to adapt to a simpler system than vice versa. And a person who likes hidden storage will have an easier time adapting to having everything out than someone who tends to forget what's behind closed doors would have adapting to hidden storage. I prefer Nothing Out and am a Detailed Organizer (making me a NODO) for many things. But I live with Everything Out + Simple Organizers (EOSO), so I organized the kitchen to be easy to use for them. For example, we have open shelving in the kitchen for our dishes. But I make it pleasant for me by having all white dishes, so the piles and stacks still look okay out in the open. And the drawers have smaller dividers inside them, so they are not chaotic. They're simple, open containers inside a larger drawer, so they're not too complicated for the Simple Organizers in the house to just toss stuff in.

If you have more than one Organizing Personality in your home, your own spaces can be organized for your own Organizing Personality. But the organizational systems in your common family areas should cater to the Everything Out + Simple Organizers (EOSO) in your house. For example, if you lean toward the Nothing Out + Detailed Organizer personality, but your family members do not, your own office and bedroom can be filled with lidded containers behind closed doors to your heart's content. But the common areas, like the kitchen, family room, and bathrooms, should probably have open shelves and large clear containers with plenty of labeling so *everyone* easily knows where things go.

Use the worksheet on the next page to find your Organizing Personality. And if you want visual examples of the way the different Organizing Personalities store and organize their things, make sure you grab yourself *The Clutter Fix* bonus at HomeMadeLovely.com /tcfbonus, which includes links to Pinterest boards filled with ideas for each personality type. Then read on to find out more about sentimental clutter and how you can keep your memories . . . *with less stuff.*

What's Your Organizing Personality? Quiz

Take the quiz below to get a general sense of which Organizing Personality *may* fit you. Or if you prefer, take our online Organizing Personality quiz at HomeMadeLovely.com/organizing-personality-quiz. Then reread the description of each Organizing Personality in the chapter and decide if it sounds like the right fit. If it doesn't, either retake the quiz and refine your answers or read the other personality descriptions in chapter 5 to see which one fits better.

For each of the following three questions, circle your answer. Then add up the points for each one to get your total score. See below for your Organizing Personality.

1. I prefer containers that are:

   a. Wire or clear basket or bin—I need to see what's inside at a glance and be able to toss things in easily. **5 points**

   b. Wire or clear containers of all shapes and sizes—I want to be very organized, but I want to see my things too. **10 points**

   c. Solid with NO lid—I don't want to see the mess, but I do want easy access. **15 points**

   d. Solid with a lid—I don't want to see the contents, and I'm good with having to take off the lid to put things away. **20 points**

2. Do you prefer to see your items on shelves, or have them hidden from view behind closed doors?

   a. I need to see them! Out of sight equals out of mind, and I may forget what I have put away. **10 points**

   b. Having everything put away immediately gives me peace. **20 points**

3. Do you prefer detailed storage or simple storage?

   a. I would rather just be able to toss things into a big container and be done. **5 points**

   b. I like categories and subcategories. Give me all the little containers. **10 points**

Up to 20 points: You are an Everything Out + Simple Organizer

You prefer to see all your things because out of sight equals out of mind. You're okay with visual abundance, and you're a big-picture thinker, not into details.

20 to 30 points: You're an Everything Out + Detailed Organizer

You like to see your things, and you like visual abundance, but you also want things to be very organized. You're detail-oriented and are down to sort things into smaller categories.

30 to 40 points: You're a Nothing Out + Simple Organizer

You love, love, love to tuck things away behind closed doors, and you adore visual simplicity. Your storage and organizational systems need to be easy-to-use because you are so not into details.

40 to 50 points: You're a Nothing Out + Detailed Organizer

You are the traditional organizer. You like things hidden away, and you love smaller organization and subcategories of organization. Organizing stores and lidded containers are your jam, baby.

CHAPTER 6

How to Handle
Sentimental Things

W e've touched on sentimental clutter several times already, but we're finally going to dive into it a bit deeper here. Whether you're consciously aware of it or not, if your home is cluttered, it's very likely that at least some of the clutter is made up of sentimental clutter. *Sentimental clutter is clutter that you've knowingly or, more likely, unknowingly assigned emotional value to and are holding on to for this reason and not because it's actually useful to your life.* This can happen with items you genuinely like and items that you really don't like but feel attached to nonetheless.

So why is sentimental clutter so hard for us to let go of? Well, according to Julie Holland, MD, an assistant clinical professor of psychiatry at New York University School of Medicine, "Sentimental clutter is the adult equivalent of a teddy bear."[1] A study from the Yale School of Medicine found that "for many, letting go is literally painful"[2]—meaning that for some of us, parts of our brain associated with psychological pain are triggered when trying to part with certain items. Conversely, holding on to this sentimental clutter is somewhat comforting. But as Julia Brenner so aptly said in her Apartment Therapy article back in 2017, "When the items are no longer being used or enjoyed, I'm not really preserving anything. . . . I'm just hanging onto them. And *hanging on is different than preserving.*"[3]

Just because you may find it difficult mentally and even physically to give up these sentimental items, as many people do, doesn't mean you should hold on to all of them and allow them to clutter up your home and life forevermore—causing more *daily* pain from the stress of too much clutter. *You can keep the memories without all the stuff.*

Let's look at a few ways you can actually feel good about parting with sentimental clutter.

Less Is Different Than None

Keeping sentimental items is not a bad thing. Let me repeat that—*it is not bad or wrong to keep things that remind you of a person, experience, or accomplishment.* Holding on to sentimental items only becomes negative when you don't have the space to do so, and the clutter begins to affect your home and life. Often, all the items from family members, memorabilia, and other sentimental things (plus the sheer volume of these things collected over time) can become overwhelming. So, we shove them away in a corner in a box . . . and then feel stressed by the pile each time we pass by. What if, instead of squirreling away all these things, you kept a select few items that most remind you of the person or experience you'd like to remember?

> **A decluttered home matters because**
>
> "When your home is clutter-free, you actually have more space in your mind to think and be creative. It is also important to me because it helps us to function more efficiently in our day-to-day goings-on."

For example, my grandmother's beautiful china lived in a box at my sister's until I had room for it. Even when I did decide that I had the room for it, I chose to pare it down and *not* keep every single piece. Rather than keeping a large random number of each dish (a result of decades of use and the occasionally inevitable broken dish), I chose to keep eight complete place settings, as well as one platter, one serving bowl, and the creamer and sugar bowl. That is far fewer pieces than I was originally given, but just the right amount so that we can store and *use* the dishes when we set the table for family dinners. The memories of my grandmother are still present, but I now don't have to store, clean, or maintain more than we will actually use. And the dishes are now a joy instead of a burden. (Except for when we have to hand-wash them because they can't go in the dishwasher. That's not quite so joyful.)

When paring back your sentimental clutter, you could also choose to keep a few items in a memorabilia box (which we'll talk about a bit more in chapter 14), like special baby clothes or a preserved flower and the invitation from your wedding day, for example.

Less is not the same as none.

Removing the Item Doesn't Remove the Memory

While the items in our home may remind us of or prompt a memory, removing the item doesn't take away the memory. *If you need to, reread that.* Our memories reside in our minds and, metaphorically speaking, in our hearts. They do not live in the things themselves. You do not have to keep the thing to feel the feelings.

If it helps you, take a photo of the thing that prompts the memory, so that you can choose to look at it again whenever you wish without the stress and strain of storing it, tripping over it, or cleaning it.

You don't have to keep the thing to keep the memory.

Saying Goodbye Can Be a Good Thing

This advice comes from Marie Kondo, author of *The Life-Changing Magic of Tidying Up.* We are human beings who find goodbyes difficult, but often necessary for closure. If we take the time to hold each sentimental thing with great memories attached to it and review the memory, being thankful for what it was at that time in our lives and saying goodbye to it before parting with it, it will be easier to let go of the thing and move on.[4]

Saying goodbye can provide a healthy sense of closure.

Create a Designated Space for Storing Sentimental Items and Stick to It

One way to control how much sentimental stuff you keep in your home is to set actual physical limits like I did with my grandmother's china—it has to fit in the glass door cabinet with our other serving dishes with no overflow anywhere else in the house. Joanna Gaines did this with each of her kids' baby clothes when she kept a few select items for each kiddo in a separate box with a note for each of them "in case they are sentimental like their momma."[5] You can do something similar for kids' artwork and schoolwork, your yearbooks (are those still a thing?) and school transcripts, and any other items you really want to hang on to.

Limit the space you give sentimental things, so you remain in control of the items in your home.

Make Room for More Memories

Sentimental items remind us of people, events, and accomplishments—all the important things in life. But if all those things we collect over the years keep us from experiencing more of those important life things now, shouldn't we clear a path for making new memories? Clutter can pile up and keep us from experiencing new things and spending time with the people we love because we're so busy managing it or because we're too embarrassed to share our life and home with others because of the mess.

Don't let the burden of yesterday's memories keep you from experiencing new ones.

Finally, dear one, remember that *what you decide to save and keep is a very personal decision.* Be brave and know that *you don't have to keep everything.* You aren't tossing the memories when you pass on the things. You simply don't need all of the physical stuff. And I will reiterate that you should choose to face the sentimental clutter after you've gotten rid of the easier stuff.

Use the worksheet at the end of this chapter to work through how you're going to handle your sentimental clutter.

A Quick Word about Hoarding

Before we move on, I want to point out that hoarding is different from simply hanging on to sentimental items. Much like sentimental clutter keepers, though, hoarders have trouble letting go of their things. They refuse to donate, trash, or sell things, and the thought of doing so causes them great distress. Hoarders' piles of stuff also tend to make living space dangerous, and moving around in their homes is very difficult due to the sheer volume of things.

According to GoodTherapy.org,

Hoarding is a serious mental health condition that can expose people who do it to dangerous living conditions, the derision of family and friends, and social isolation. About 5% of the world's population hoards, but only about 15% of people who hoard recognize that their behavior is irrational.[6]

If you believe that you or someone you love has a hoarding issue, first of all, know that you and they are loved. We were all created by our Father God, who cares about us beyond comprehension. Second, seek out help. Find a godly therapist or counselor in your area who has experience dealing with hoarding and reach out to them.

Dealing with Your Sentimental Items

1. Do you have any sentimental items that you're holding on to in your home?

   ☐ Yes   ☐ No

2. What are those items and who are they from?

3. Think about each of the items you listed above. Why are you keeping each one? Be really honest. Is it out of guilt? Fear of what someone will say if you don't keep it? Or because you genuinely love and/or use that item?

4. Do you have room to store or display each of those items properly, without causing excess clutter in your home? Or do you need to find another way to remember and honor the person who gave you each item?

5. For each item, write down what you will do with it: Keep it as is and make room for it by clearing out other items, preserve the memory with a photo of the item, or just get rid of it and let the memory live in your head.

CHAPTER 7

How to Get Your Family on Board—*or Not*

Okay, lovely, the reason this chapter is called "How to Get Your Family on Board—*Or Not*" is that the honest-to-goodness truth is that *you may **not** be able to get everyone on board with decluttering*. While decluttering, like anything related to the upkeep of the home, is obviously easier when everyone works together (many hands make light work, and all that), and I do believe everyone who lives in a house (men, women, and children alike) *should* help with the household chores, it doesn't always happen that way.

So, what exactly do you do if your spouse, siblings, roommates, or kids have zero interest in decluttering or organizing, and they're dragging their feet, kicking, and screaming as you try to make progress in the home you all share? Read on to find out.

Your Spouse, Your Roommate, or Any Other Adult in Your House

It happens all the time. One person in a house gets tired of all the clutter and wants to do something about it. The other person is happy with the status quo (or they don't want to face the work of declut-tering). So, frustration sets in, and decluttering becomes a point of contention rather than a means to achieve a more peaceful home. It can be especially frustrating when your housemates aren't as excited about decluttering as you are. So, what do you do if they just don't get it? Or see why it's necessary? What do you do when you just want to create a simpler home, but they are not on board? Well, lovely, *you do not need them to be on board.* You don't. Would it be easier? Maybe. Is it necessary? Nope.

I do not want you to procrastinate or put off decluttering and or-ganizing just because another person in your home doesn't want to do it with you. *Do not let their inaction keep you from making progress.* Their refusal to help is not a valid excuse anymore. You can purge and streamline and simplify your home anyway. You can create peaceful, clutter-free spaces. *You don't have to get them on board!*

Here are a few ways to go about decluttering when someone else in your house isn't keen on all this decluttering and organizing stuff.

1. Don't declutter their stuff without permission. You will never win them over if you start tossing their stuff. Leave well enough alone. Make progress elsewhere in the house so they can see how much it makes a difference in your peace and in the peace of the household and maybe—just maybe—they will want to participate in future de-cluttering sessions.

2. Find out why they are hesitant. Have an honest discussion about why they don't want to declutter. What is it exactly that they have an issue with? Refer back to the Clutter Personalities in chapter 4, and find out if they're a Worrywart or a Wishful Thinker or maybe a De-layer. Help them to discover why they are reluctant to part with things. Don't attack them for what they believe or feel. But have a genuine, honest conversation about it. You may find it very enlightening and gain some insight as to ways you could potentially help them and get them on board.

3. Lead by example and focus on your own belongings. Purge and clear out your own things. Set up organizational systems in the common areas that work for everyone in the house (make sure you read chapter 5 for help with this), and then work on maintaining your own stuff. Sometimes all it takes is seeing how much more peace and calm simplification can add to bring someone around to the idea of decluttering.

4. Set common goals to work toward. Talk about how purging will leave more time and space for more important things. Think about rewards such as not being embarrassed to have people over, or clearing out a junk room to make way for a pool table, or simply having more time to spend doing fun things rather than cleaning and tidying. Or choose whatever common goals would make everyone happy. Then work toward those together.

5. Help them by giving them the tools they need. Make sure you have boxes for donating things and trash bags for tossing stuff while they're purging. Set up organization systems that will work for them too (again see chapter 5 for more on this). Make it easy for *them*. For example, if you like Nothing Out + Detailed Organization (everything in lidded containers behind closed doors) but the other people in your house are Everything Out + Simple Organizers (EOSO), you will likely never get them to organize the way *you* want. It just goes against their natural tendencies. Instead, organize rooms that you all share so that it's easy for them to find and put things away. In the bathroom, for instance, rather than putting all the lotions

> **A decluttered home matters because**
>
> "A decluttered, lovely home is peaceful and welcoming. Proverb 24:3-4 says, 'By wisdom a house is built, and through understanding it is established; through knowledge its rooms are filled with rare and beautiful treasures.' I desire anything I have to be meaningful and make my heart feel happy."

and soaps in a cabinet sorted by type, keep them out in the open where they can be seen and used easily. But put them in a low-sided tray so you don't lose your ever-loving mind because there are bottles everywhere. Work with them to make organization easy.

6. Be patient and show grace. It may take time—a long time—to get someone else on board. Or they may never get it. That's okay. It just is—*because it has to be.* The end goal is to create an atmosphere of peace and calm in your home, not just reduce the amount of stuff in it. Don't give up on hoping they will come around, but don't put off simplifying while you wait for them to maybe, possibly, get on board.

7. **Show gratitude** and offer words of encouragement and appreciation if and when they do put some work into decluttering. People like to hear how much you appreciate them, and the other adults in your house are certainly no exception. (Think about how you would feel if they told you how much they appreciated the work you were doing. See? Praise and gratitude can go a long way.)

8. **Schedule regular decluttering sessions.** Gently let it be known that you purge the toys every year around the holidays. Or that you clean out the shed every spring. Add decluttering to the shared household calendar. Regularly including decluttering in your routines will help it to feel like it's not random or haphazard, or a passing trend that comes at anyone out of left field.

9. **Create one space that is your own** and keep it clutter-free just for you. **Or do the opposite and negotiate just one or two spaces the other person can treat however they like,** like the garage or the office. Then you can declutter the remaining spaces to your heart's content. Allie Casazza, another mom who teaches about decluttering and simplifying, tells a story on her podcast of how her husband, Brian, wasn't initially on board with her desire for minimalism. So, they negotiated the garage and one other space that he could keep however he wanted. They went along tickety-boo for a couple of years that way. Then when they were moving, and she packed up the whole house in a couple of days at eight months pregnant, they had to delay the movers because he took so long with his spaces. That was when he decided that simplifying was totally worth it.[1]

Your Kids

Okay, so we've talked about what to do if the other adults in your home aren't interested in decluttering. But if you have children, what about them? What if they're giving you pushback on all this decluttering and organizing? Well, guess what? Your kids are not the boss; *you are*. The Bible says to "train up a child in the way he should go: and when he is old, he will not depart from it" (Proverbs 22:6 KJV). Which, among other things, means that you get to decide when and where to declutter and how the house should function. I don't mean you should run roughshod over their things and start tossing things left and right from underneath them. But you do get to lead here and set the tone for the organization in your home. Here are a few ways to help your kids with the decluttering process.

1. Start small and don't overwhelm them. If you've seemingly not cared one lick about the clutter before now and your house has always been messy, this whole decluttering thing will be an adjustment for your kids. Start decluttering and organizing small by focusing on common areas, or just a closet even. Help them to purge by being there to support them and by showing them how to evaluate what should stay and what should go (refer to chapter 10 if you need help with this).

2. Be compassionate and respectful of their spaces, such as their bedrooms. Let them make some decisions in those spaces. Older kids should be given some extra leeway here. Worst-case scenario, they don't do anything to clean up, and you simply go into their room as little as possible from now on. At first, it will be hard, and you may feel very annoyed. I know how you feel. Dean and I have three kids, and even now as young adults, one will tidy their room when reminded and do a great job, one needs no reminding and keeps their room super tidy and organized, and one (our Creative) couldn't care less about tidiness and has stuff *everywhere*. After years of butting heads with the messy-room child, I gave up, and now that she's a young adult I just don't go into her room unless it's necessary. Our relationship means more to me than arguing over a messy room. "Pick your battles" is a cliché for a reason.

3. Consider that it may just be a phase. Young children have a "tendency to become strongly attached to inanimate objects, usually soft, cuddly toys or blankets."[2] During this developmental stage, show extra grace and let them keep things that seem to matter a lot to them, even if you don't understand why.

When our youngest was about four or five years old, we were purging and cleaning out the house by holding a garage sale. I had decluttered all three of the kids' toys and books and collected things I thought they never used. One such item was a small, cheap stuffed blue elephant (belonging to our youngest) that we'd won at a fair or something. I had no idea until after I'd sold it with several other stuffed animals that she loved it so much. She cried and asked for it for ages. And even years later I feel sad knowing that I made her sad by getting rid of something so small that really wasn't taking up that much room at all. If I'd known then what I know now, I'd have let her keep it. Once you purge and clean up the rest of the house, it really won't matter if you let the kids keep a few extra things that you don't see the point of but that seem special to them.

4. Give them less stuff. Kids need much less stuff than you think, and there are plenty of ways to love on them without adding clutter to your home in the form of more stuff. Spend time with them, playing games or reading books together. Go on adventures together. Don't default to buying things for every birthday, holiday, and celebration, and you won't have anywhere near as much stuff to manage.

5. Don't maintain their stuff for them once they're old enough to do it for themselves. *If they're old enough to give you pushback in any form about cleaning up, they're old enough to look after their own space*, and you should not be cleaning their rooms for them! I cannot reiterate this enough. Not only are you creating more work for yourself if you do this; you're also not teaching your kids how to look after themselves. Which will bite both you and them in the butt when they grow up and move out. We've always taught our kids how to pick up after them-selves, starting as soon as they could walk. We'd do the "Ten-Second Tidy" with Loonette the clown on *The Big Comfy Couch* when they were small to help them learn to pick up their toys. And now they all have to clear their own stuff from the family common areas on their own—because I have zero tolerance for messes staying in the spaces everyone shares after someone leaves the room. Do they need reminding? Yup. Do I clean it up for them? Not a chance!

6. Show gratitude and praise them when they work on decluttering their spaces or help with the family common areas. Again, people like to hear how much you appreciate them, and your kiddos are no exception. Kind words and genuine appreciation can go a long way.

Okay, so although you may or may not get the other adults in your house on board, your kids should definitely have to help declutter and keep things organized. But what about extended family or friends? How do you handle it when they just keep bringing stuff over and don't want to limit the things they give you?

Your Extended Family and Friends

With extended family and friends, the first thing you need to do is to have a chat with them if you haven't already. Use the Quick Clutter Assessment worksheet from the introduction to help you articulate what you're trying to do and why a clutter-free home is so important to you. After that, if they're still not on board and in agreement, *you need to manage your expectations.* You simply cannot expect your mom or dad or aunt or best friend to be on the same page as you. Be kind. Show grace. Perhaps stuff is how they show love—gifts are one of the five love languages, after all. Let them love on you and your family. *But* you continue to do what you wish in your own little family unit. Limit your gift-giving of things, or change them to experiences and creating memories instead. Like Allie Casazza says, when someone gives you a gift, "it doesn't come with a secret, unspoken contract that you have to keep it for any certain amount of time. So, when somebody gives a gift and it comes into your home, that's great. Be gracious. Be kind. Be

> **A decluttered home matters because**
>
> "It is visually calming and peaceful to not see stuff lying around. When it is organized, day-to-day items and seasonal items can easily be found."

thankful. And mean it. And then when that toy or that item runs its course and it's time to send it on to the donation center, that's fine. You shouldn't feel guilty about that."[3] Continue to purge seasonally and around major life events, as we'll talk about in chapter 14, knowing you've done what you can do as far as the people in your life go in relation to stuff and clutter.

Use the worksheet on the following pages to create a plan for handling clutter that comes from your family and friends. Then, let's get your mind in line with your home goals before we begin to purge the clutter from your home.

Friends and Family and the Clutter in Your Home

1. Do you have family members or friends who contribute to the clutter in your home? If yes, who (spouse, kids, mom, dad, your bestie)?

   ☐ Yes   ☐ No

   _____

   _____

2. If you answered yes to question 1, in what way do they cause clutter? Do they bring in too many things? Do they give you things they don't want? Or do they just not tidy up after themselves?

   _____

   _____

   _____

3. Do you have other people in your home who don't want to declutter or part with things? If yes, who?

   ☐ Yes   ☐ No

   _____

   _____

   _____

4. If they don't want to declutter, why do you think that is? Does this seem to be coming out of the blue becausee you have not cared about clutter before? Are there systems in place yet to make tidying and organizing simple for them? Are they young and simply going through a phase?

   _____

   _____

   _____

5. If you answered yes to either question 1 or question 3, jot down ideas for getting them on board with your decluttering. What would make it easier for them to want to participate? Use the ideas in this chapter to inspire your own ideas.

_____

_____

_____

6. Connect with the family and friends that you need to chat with, and set up a time to discuss your plans. When will this happen?

_____

_____

_____

Hopefully they will be on board after your discussion. But if they aren't, make a promise with yourself that you will declutter and organize anyway.

CHAPTER 8

Five Decluttering
Mindset Hacks

L isten, I know that decluttering isn't the most fun task in the world. It can feel overwhelming when we don't know where to start, and decluttering takes time. It's messy and it's hard work. When you feel like you're stuck or overwhelmed, you've got to remember why you're doing this. "Clutter is not just the stuff on your floor—it's anything that stands between you and the life you want to be living."[1] And all that clutter is keeping you from having the peaceful, calm, stress-free home you so badly want and need. It needs to go. "Eliminate the unnecessary so that the necessary may speak."[2]

Even when we know we desperately need to declutter and get our homes organized, it can be hard to keep the momentum going so we can get the job done. We can get distracted and frustrated because we have to make more messes before it gets better. We can't always see the end results in our head, and we get bogged down in the middle of the purging. Our brains need a little help to keep going. That's why I'm sharing these five mindset hacks with you. I want you to practice them and keep them in mind as we move on to the more comprehensive, room-by-room decluttering and then to the blessed maintenance mode in the rest of the book.

1. Do NOT Tackle Sentimental Stuff First

It's just harder. Wait until you have some other things cleared out. Until you have a little practice exercising your decluttering muscles. Then you can take the time to sit with your memories and make decisions about what to keep and what not to. When you're ready to deal with sentimental clutter, revisit chapter 6.

2. Take Before and After Photos for Motivation

A majorly motivating trick that I love to use when decorating and de-cluttering is to take before and after photos. I learned this in the early days of my blog. Anytime we did a project, I'd take before and after photos to share with our readers. And while, of course, our readers loved them (who doesn't love a good before and after!), I found myself looking at those photos again and again as motivation for the next project.

> A decluttered home matters because
>
> "It makes me feel more sane and less overwhelmed."

If you take before shots of all the clutter and then new photos of the decluttered spaces from the same angle as you declutter, you will *really* see the difference you've made. This will help you get motivated to keep going in your other spaces. And this will also help you stay motivated to keep the clutter cleared out!

3. Focus on the Type of Person You Want to Be Versus the Act of Decluttering

In his book *Atomic Habits*, James Clear talks about "identity-based habits,"[3] meaning that we should focus on the person we wish to become, not what we want to achieve. So, the goal wouldn't be to have a clutter-free home; the goal would be to be a person who puts things away as soon as you're done with them. We'll talk more about building these habits in chapter 14. But for now, think about becoming the type of person who looks after their things, not necessarily about having a perfectly tidy home.

4. Ask Yourself What You Want to KEEP Instead of What You Want to Get Rid Of

Sometimes a tiny mindset shift is all it takes to push us over the edge into new habits and new ways of doing things. This is true for the task of decluttering too.

When you're decluttering, instead of focusing on all that you're getting rid of and what you must part with, try *focusing on the things you want to keep*. The things that will bring you joy. The things you are willing to dust and clean because you love them so much. Focus on these rather than on all the stuff you just feel ho-hum about that is currently sapping your energy.

5. Use Affirmations to Help You Change Your Mindset

Before you worry that I'm getting all woo-woo or new age-y on you, let me reassure you that affirmations do not have to be weird. They're simply a way to consistently remind yourself to think specific good things. "They're a statement or proposition that is declared to be true."[4] They're a tool you can use to help you reach your peaceful home goals.

As Joyce Meyer says, "You cannot have a positive life and a negative mind."[5] Affirmations help you because they make you more aware of negative thoughts, they have the potential to change what you think and believe about yourself, and they can help you to feel more positive, energetic, and motivated. They are a powerful tool in rewiring old thought patterns and creating new, more positive thought pathways. These in turn lead to better habits and actions in our lives.

> Good thoughts and actions can never produce bad results; bad thoughts and actions can never produce good results.
>
> James Allen, *As a Man Thinketh*

As he thinketh in his heart, so is he.

Proverbs 23:7 KJV

In many places, the Bible also mentions the importance of being aware and careful of what we think about. Here are two verses that stand out in my mind:

Whatever is true, whatever is honorable, whatever is just, whatever is pure, whatever is lovely, whatever is commendable, if there is any excellence, if there is anything worthy of praise, think about these things.

Philippians 4:8 ESV

Do not be conformed to this world, but be transformed by the renewal of your mind, that by testing you may discern what is the will of God, what is good and acceptable and perfect.

Romans 12:2 ESV

In both passages, the apostle Paul encourages us not to get sucked into negative thinking but to bring our minds back to just, pure, and lovely thoughts, *deliberately*! We do this when we study Bible verses and read uplifting stories of faith and perseverance. And we can also do this by creating and focusing on positive words of affirmation regularly.

What you think with your mind changes your brain and body, and you are designed with the power to switch on your brain. Your mind is that switch. You have an extraordinary ability to determine, achieve, and maintain optimal levels of intelligence, mental health, peace, and happiness, as well as the prevention of disease in your body and mind. You can, through conscious effort, gain control of your thoughts and feelings, and in doing so, you can change the programming and chemistry of your brain.[6]

Words are mightily powerful. And we can use them to help us with our clutter, just as we can use them to help us with weight loss, finances, faith, and even encouraging our loved ones.

So, What Are Affirmations?

Affirmations can be as simple as a few words strung together into a sentence or phrase that you find meaningful. They can be Bible verses, song lyrics, or quotes from your favorite author or book. Whatever words you feel will help you to make changes in your life and home. Generally speaking, you need to believe the words of affirmation in order for them to help your thought patterns. So, saying random things like "I am rich beyond my wildest dreams," as some suggest for wealth affirmations, is likely to fall flat if you're struggling to make ends meet. Instead, focus on where you are at now and the next logical step, and choose your affirmations accordingly. As you find yourself thinking positive thoughts more regularly, you can "uplevel" your affirmations to bigger ones.

How Do You Use Affirmations?

Once you've decided on the phrases or sentences that speak to you and where you're at in a particular season of your decluttering and organization, choose a few and keep them front and center in any of the following ways:

- Writing them out daily in your journal
- Putting them on notes where you'll see them throughout your day (like on your bathroom mirror, your desk, or your car's dashboard)
- Keeping a list on your phone or by your bed and simply reading through them before you fall asleep or when you wake up each morning

35+ Affirmations to Get You Started

To get you started with good affirmations, here are thirty-five affirmations that you may find helpful, both in decluttering your home and generally improving your mental outlook on life (which, of course, extends into your home as well). I've also included some space for you to jot down a few of your own:

1. Less is more.
2. I am making progress.
3. It feels good to let things go.
4. I am moving toward a lovelier, more peaceful home.
5. I will be gentle with myself when I'm decluttering.
6. Done is better than perfect.
7. I am enjoying more space in my home.
8. I am happy even when I don't buy more stuff.
9. I will have what I need when I need it.
10. I can't take it with me.
11. Amassing material things is not the point of life.
12. "God is within her, she will not fall" (Psalm 46:5).
13. I am a child of God.
14. I am smart, capable, and talented.
15. I am creative because I was made in the image of the Creator.
16. I easily let go of things that no longer serve me.
17. I enjoy living an organized and clutter-free life.
18. I always know where my _____ is because my home is neat and clutter-free.
19. I am ready, willing, and able to change my relationship with clutter.
20. I love living in a clutter-free environment.
21. People and relationships are more important than things.
22. I enjoy living a simple life.
23. "And God is able to bless you abundantly, so that in all things at all times, having all that you need, you will abound in every good work" (2 Corinthians 9:8).

24. "Do not be anxious about anything, but in every situation, by prayer and petition, with thanksgiving, present your requests to God" (Philippians 4:6).
25. Having space in my home (office, car, etc.) allows me to think clearly.
26. If I haven't needed it in a year, I don't need it.
27. I love being organized.
28. Being organized allows me to do more in life.
29. Living in a clean house makes me feel good.
30. My home is an extension of my life, which is neat and organized.
31. I do not need to own a lot of stuff.
32. My possessions do not define me.
33. If I need it later, I can buy it later.
34. I am grateful for my simple life.
35. I find security in God, rather than in the things I own.

Write your own below.

_____

_____

_____

Tip: It helps if your affirmations are worded in the first person: "I" instead of "you," and so on. Of course, you can keep Bible verses as they are written.

As you declutter and begin to work on achieving a clutter-free home, I highly encourage you to try some of these affirmations—or simply "positive words," if you rather—to get and keep you on the right track.

As we close out this section on building a decluttering mindset, it's important to note that there is no unending space. We all have space constraints and can't keep everything. It doesn't matter whether you live in five hundred square feet or two thousand square feet (or more). Think of your house like a container with a limit to its capacity. You don't have to fill it all with stuff! Nor do you have to manage all that "inventory." Just as leaving some white space in your calendar is good for your soul, leaving some white space in your home is good for you too. Consider this my daring you to try it!

Keep these five mindset hacks front and center in your mind. Especially practice the affirmations as you declutter the rest of the house and then master the routines you need to keep your home clutter-free. I'd love to see what affirmations speak most to you. Share the ones that inspire you on social media using the hashtag #theclutterfix.

PART 3

DECLUTTER and ORGANIZE EVERY ROOM in YOUR HOME

CHAPTER 9

How to Purge and Organize Your Entire House in Seven Simple Steps

Everything in your home should have a space, an assigned home, where it "lives." There shouldn't be any stragglers or random things lying around. It should be easy for you to straighten up at the end of the day or before someone comes to visit. Your home will still get messy, but those messes will be oh-so-much easier to clean up. Steve McClatchy puts it this way, which I absolutely love: "Everyone has a place in their house for forks. If you found a random fork in the bathroom or under the couch, you'd immediately know it didn't belong there and would return it to its drawer without another thought. Everything in your life should be this easy to put away. If an item occupies no specific location when not in use, it becomes clutter."[1] This is why we organize our homes—to make it easy to keep our stuff under control. Remember, it's all about creating a calm, peaceful home in which to live our wonderful lives. "Having a simplified, uncluttered home is a form of self-care."[2]

In chapter 12, I will give you very specific instructions for purging and organizing each room and space in your home, right down to every last drawer and cupboard. The seven steps below are the bones of those specifics, and I'm outlining them here so that you see a pattern: *All decluttering and organizing follows these same seven steps.*

1. Empty and Sort

Remove everything from the space you're trying to organize. If you get overwhelmed easily, empty and sort one small section (like a single drawer or shelf) at a time. Dump it all out. Create a huge pile if necessary. Then start sorting. Place like with like. Don't try to be tidy with this. The mess actually has to get worse before it can get better.

If you're cleaning a playroom, for example, make little heaps of toy cars, dinosaurs, dolls, etc. If it's the kitchen pantry, put all the crackers, cereal, soup, etc., in their own "piles."

2. Purge, Edit, and Eliminate

After your things are sorted, decide what you want to keep and what you don't. Get rid of anything that's broken and unworthy of fixing. Next, donate to local and national nonprofits any items that are in good shape but that you haven't used in a while. Then sort by season, color, name, or any other way you wish to organize what's left in a particular space. (Refer to chapter 10 for help deciding what to purge and what to keep, and to chapter 2 for specific places to get rid of your clutter.)

3. Assign Everything a Home

All the items you decided to keep need to have a specific place or home within your home. *Just like the forks do.* Once you have sorted and eliminated unwanted items, you should have a pretty good idea of how much space you need for each grouping. Assign homes in cupboards and on shelves for these things. Assign the things you use often to places within easy reach. Things that are used infrequently can go up higher or in a slightly less accessible spot.

Refer to the Organizing Personalities in chapter 5 when you're working on this step, remembering to keep things simple for everyone.

4. Shop for Bins, Baskets, and Containers

After your "keep items" have an assigned place, you can shop for pretty containers, baskets, labels, or whatever you need to get and stay organized. This step is my personal favorite because I love shopping and organizing. But be sure to do it after the first three steps have been completed. You don't truly know what bins or baskets you need until you have sorted, eliminated, and assigned homes for your things. It's also a bit of a puzzle to figure out what fits where. *Make sure you measure the height, width, and depth of shelves and cupboards before buying containers*—it's no fun to choose pretty containers only to realize they don't fit the way you thought they would.

Don't forget to shop your own house too for containers to corral all the mess and then check places like the dollar store and craft store for some great storage solutions. And if money is tight, you can even use cardboard boxes wrapped in plain Kraft paper, wrapping paper, or wallpaper.

> "Clutter is the stuff that is keeping our homes from being what we need them to be. Clutter is too much and too many. Too many toys. Too many clothes. Too many things to do on a Saturday morning. Clutter complicates life without adding anything to it. Clutter is the meaningless getting in the way of the meaningful."
>
> —KELLY ORIBINE

Also, remember to keep in mind your Organizing Personality when shopping for organization containers. You'll want to choose containers that will work *for* you and the other people in your house, not against you. For example, Everything Outs + Simple Organizers (EOSO) will prefer clear containers on open shelves, while Nothing Outs + Detailed Organizers (NODO) love many containers behind closed doors.

Tip: Get The Clutter Fix *free bonus printables at HomeMadeLovely .com/tcfbonus and use* The Clutter Fix *grid paper to sketch your spaces and plot out your organization.*

5. Label It and Put It All Away

No matter what the Organizing Personality, labels are everyone's best friend. They are especially helpful in keeping things organized with multiple people in a house. Use a Cricut to make pretty labels or use a label maker for simple labels. Heck, you can even use a piece of masking tape and a marker if money is tight (try cutting the tape straight, rather than tearing it off the roll, to make it look tidy). Be sure to label everything so that you and everyone else in your house know where to put things away when they're finished with them.

6. Maintain, Maintain, Maintain

After purging and organizing, you will need to put things in their place when you are finished with them. If you can't put things back right away, make sure you do it at the end of every day. It shouldn't take more than five to ten minutes in each room to get everything back in its place once it has a home. You just have to do it. (I'll tell you how to make this oh-so-much easier with routines and habits in part 4.)

I'm one of those people who has finally—honestly, after years of not doing it—decided it's much better for my personal sanity to come down to a tidy kitchen in the morning. It means that, yes, we're loading dishes into the dishwasher and wiping down counters before bed when we're tired (because we have teenagers and young adults living here,

I feel like we do this a thousand times a day!), but it also means that my morning doesn't feel like it's started "behind the eight-ball" so to speak, in a mess. I also put away the remotes and fluff the pillows on the couch in the living room before bed every night too. It just makes me smile to wake up to an organized and pretty version of our spaces in the morning. *And now that I've done it for so long, it's just a reflex to do it before heading up to bed.*

7. Change Systems if Needed

If something in your new organizing system isn't working for you or your family after you set it up, give yourself the grace and permission to change it. There's no need to force anyone to comply with a system that just doesn't work for them or the space. Just tweak the basics that you've started with as you find you need to.

For example, we used to keep our spices in small mason jars on a tiered rack on the huge rolling pantry shelves that Dean made for our last kitchen (perfect for the Everything Out + Simple Organizers (EOSO) in our house). But after we renovated our current house's kitchen, there wasn't room for that rack anywhere in the space, so we switched our spice storage to small picture ledges on the wall by the stove instead. The basics of our spice organization still worked in the form of the jars out in the open, but we needed to tweak how they were stored in a way that still worked for our people and the room.

You could do something similar if you've tried, for example, spices tucked in a drawer, but find they need to be visible. Or if you store all your craft supplies in tiny opaque containers but never use them because you can't see them, or you never tidy up because it's too much work to sort items into individual containers. Set up systems, but adjust as needed.

Okay, that's the method I use throughout our house, and that's the method I'm going to refer to when we are working on each room with more specifics. First, though, we will go through how to decide what to keep and what to get rid of in the next chapter.

CHAPTER 10

How to Decide What to Get Rid of and What to Keep

Very soon we're going to begin to tackle all the rooms in your home to free them of their clutter. But how do you decide what to part with and what to keep when doing that? That's what we're going to take a look at in this chapter, so you know what to do ahead of time.

As you're going through your rooms and spaces decluttering them step-by-step in chapter 12, you need to ask yourself these three clarifying questions about the things you're sorting:

1. Is It Beautiful?

Of course, we don't *just* want a clutter-free home. We want one that is lovely and beautiful too. If you love something because it's beautiful— like you'd actually go out and purchase it in the store today—and you have the space for it, it can stay. Beautiful things are a joy and delight in this sometimes-dreary world. It's totally okay to keep pretty things in your home, just because they're pretty and they fill you with happiness when you see them, as long as they're not adding to the clutter. It's better to keep a few lovely things than it is to fill your house to the brim. Also, keep in mind that beauty is subjective. So, what I may find beautiful, you may not. And vice versa. Only you can decide the answer to this question in your house.

2. Is It Useful?

There are a few things that can *just* be beautiful in your home, but there will be many more things that serve a purpose. They are useful items. *If you genuinely need something, it can stay.*

Along with this question, there is the additional, follow-up question of "Is this the *only thing* that can be useful in its way?" If you have somehow collected four snow shovels over the years, they're *technically* all useful . . . but you probably don't need all of them! Get rid of the extras and keep the best one.

Keep what is useful, but not in excess. Remember, you have what you need right now, and God will provide for what you need in the future.

3. Is It Sentimental?

Sentimental clutter keeps coming up again and again, doesn't it? *Is it sentimental?* can be a bit of a tricky question to answer because of the emotions we often attach to sentimental items. As I mentioned in chapter 6, my grandmother's china is lovely. It's classic white bone china with a gold rim. It's beautiful and it means something because it was my grandma's. But until recently, I truly didn't have the space for it, so it lived in a tote in my sister's basement until I had room for it. If you have something sentimentally similar, you will need to decide whether to keep it depending on space and how much it truly means to you (or whether the memories alone are enough). The sentimental question is something *only* you can answer. But you have to ask yourself, *Am I keeping something out of guilt or a sense of obligation? Or a genuine desire to keep it?* Do you need to keep the actual item, or will a photo of it suffice? (Refer back to chapter 6 again if you find that you need help when decluttering sentimental items.)

CHAPTER 11

Three Methods of Decluttering— *and the Right One for You in This Season*

I know with the pace of life with kids and jobs, it can be really hard to find time to clean and declutter. Especially when there are so many more fun and necessary things to do! And sometimes other things like guilt or fear hold us back from decluttering too. But as we've already discussed, a clutter-free home is essential to your sanity and to the functioning of your home, so you must make time for decluttering and kick that fear to the curb! (Remember to use the affirmations from chapter 8 to help with this.)

There are three effective methods for decluttering your entire home. Each method has pros and cons and will suit different seasons of your life better than others. Read on to determine which one is right for you right now. Then choose a method and use the coordinating worksheets at the end of the chapter to prep for the room-by-room decluttering we'll do in chapter 12.

1. 10 Minutes a Day Declutter Method

For this first decluttering method, set a timer and declutter for ten minutes each day for several days. Start with the easiest spot in the house to tidy and move on from there. It will take you longer to get to a clutter-free house this way than if you use one of the other methods, but if you stay on top of it, you *will* eventually get it all done. See the included 10 Minutes a Day Declutter Method worksheet at the end of the chapter for how to do this.

A decluttered home matters because

"It makes my spirit calm and life feel more manageable, organized, and lovely. It helps me focus more on what I have to be thankful for, rather than what I don't have, or things that are distracting."

Who should use this method: People with extremely limited time and minimal clutter.

Who should not use this method: If you have a lot of clutter, this method will drag on for too long, and you may become frustrated at your lack of progress. If this is you, consider pairing this method with a weekend decluttering marathon.

2. 30-Day Whole Home Declutter Method

With the second decluttering method, you tackle the clutter and clear it out from one specific room or area in your home, every single day, for thirty days.

See the included 30-Day Whole Home Declutter Method worksheet at the end of the chapter for how to do this.

Who should use this method: People who are at home every day, or have time and energy in the evening, and can devote some time each day (for a month) to decluttering.

Who should not use this method: Moms with newborns, or those who are otherwise in a season of life that is busier or more draining than normal.

3. Whole Home in a Weekend Declutter Method

The third decluttering method is to do a decluttering marathon all at once. This method requires a little more planning. You can do your whole home in one weekend if it's small or not too cluttered. Or plan to tackle a few spaces at a time each weekend for a few weekends. But it will get you to a clutter-free home much faster.

To do a decluttering marathon you'll need to choose a weekend you're at home, with no other plans. Then you'll need to plan meals and do meal prep (or budget to order in). If you have kids, depending on their ages, you may also need childcare or other help.

See the included Weekend Marathon Prep, Weekend Decluttering Day 1, and Weekend Decluttering Day 2 worksheets at the end of the chapter to do a whole house weekend decluttering marathon.

Who should use this method: Anyone who wants to clear the clutter from their home fast and who can set aside one or more distraction-free weekends at home to do so.

Who should not use this method: Anyone with young children and no access to childcare for them for the weekend.

10 Minutes a Day Declutter Method

To declutter your whole home in ten minutes a day, you need to do a brain dump of the spaces in your home that you want to declutter. Make sure you break down larger areas into smaller bite-sized pieces. For example, the kitchen can be broken down into the pantry, fridge, freezer, countertops, drawers, cabinets, etc.

Now you need to rewrite the list in the order you want to declutter. Check each space off as you declutter it.

☐ _____ ☐ _____ ☐ _____

☐ _____ ☐ _____ ☐ _____

☐ _____ ☐ _____ ☐ _____

☐ _____ ☐ _____ ☐ _____

☐ _____ ☐ _____ ☐ _____

☐ _____ ☐ _____ ☐ _____

☐ _____ ☐ _____ ☐ _____

☐ _____ ☐ _____ ☐ _____

☐ _____ ☐ _____ ☐ _____

30-Day Whole Home Declutter Method

To declutter your whole home in thirty days, follow the daily prompts below. Refer to the in-depth instructions for each room in chapter 12 as needed.

Day 1 Outdoor porch, patio, back deck	**Day 2** Front entry and closet	**Day 3** Purses and backpacks	**Day 4** Kitchen drawers	**Day 5** Kitchen cabinets
Day 6 Kitchen table/ island	**Day 7** Pantry	**Day 8** Fridge/ freezers	**Day 9** Junk drawer	**Day 10** Dining table and hutch or buffet
Day 11 Linen closet	**Day 12** Laundry room	**Day 13** Cleaning supplies	**Day 14** Bathroom cabinets	**Day 15** Medicine cabinet
Day 16 Toiletries and makeup	**Day 17** Hair stuff and jewelry	**Day 18** Entertainment stand/area	**Day 19** Magazines and books	**Day 20** Bedroom closets
Day 21 Nightstands	**Day 22** Dressers	**Day 23** Office and desk area	**Day 24** Mail and paperwork	**Day 25** Craft space/ supplies
Day 26 Basement or attic storage	**Day 27** Garage	**Day 28** Kids' closets	**Day 29** Kids' dressers	**Day 30** Kids' toys

Weekend Marathon Prep

1. When will this happen (date)?

   _____

2. What is the plan for looking after the kids? (Are they sleeping over at grandparents? Are you getting a mother's helper to keep them out from underfoot?)

   _____

   _____

   _____

3. Where will you put the donation items from the weekend purge until you can donate them? (In the garage? In the car?)

   _____

   _____

4. Brainstorm easy meal and snack ideas to keep everyone fed while you purge.

   _____

   _____

   _____

5. Make a list of decluttering items you'll need. (Garbage bags, masking tape, markers, boxes, etc.)

   ☐ _____ ☐ _____ ☐ _____

   ☐ _____ ☐ _____ ☐ _____

   ☐ _____ ☐ _____ ☐ _____

   ☐ _____ ☐ _____ ☐ _____

6. Brainstorm all the spaces you'd ideally like to declutter.

☐ _____ ☐ _____ ☐ _____

☐ _____ ☐ _____ ☐ _____

☐ _____ ☐ _____ ☐ _____

☐ _____ ☐ _____ ☐ _____

7. Now list the spaces you plan to declutter this weekend in order of most to least important.

☐ _____   ☐ _____

☐ _____   ☐ _____

☐ _____   ☐ _____

☐ _____   ☐ _____

☐ _____   ☐ _____

☐ _____   ☐ _____

8. Add a time estimate for how long you think each will take.

Weekend Decluttering Day 1

What will you eat today?

Breakfast _____

Lunch _____

Dinner _____

Snacks _____

Which rooms will you declutter today? (Include their estimated times.)

_____   _____

_____   _____

_____   _____

_____   _____

_____   _____

_____   _____

_____   _____

_____   _____

_____   _____

_____   _____

_____   _____

Weekend Decluttering Day 2

What will you eat today?

Breakfast _____

Lunch _____

Dinner _____

Snacks _____

Which rooms will you declutter today? (Include their estimated times.)

CHAPTER 12

Step-by-Step, Room-by-Room Decluttering Guide

And finally, we get to actually decluttering your home room by room! In this section, I will walk you through each space in your home, with specific instructions to follow for decluttering that space. Regardless of the method of decluttering you chose from the last chapter (10 Minutes a Day, 30 Days, or a Weekend Marathon), these room-by-room instructions will guide you through a thorough decluttering of your home.

As you go through each space in your home, you may need the following:

☐ Boxes or labeled garbage bags to designate items as donate, toss/recycle, and sell as you go

☐ Garbage bags

☐ Pen/pencil

☐ Marker and masking tape to label garbage bags

☐ Labels

☐ Paper shredder
☐ Recycling bins
☐ Broom and dustpan or vacuum
☐ Mop
☐ Multipurpose surface spray cleaner and a cloth
☐ Paper towels
☐ Zip ties or other means of wrangling cords and wires

Follow the individual steps for each space, checking them off as you go. Then when you've done everything for a room, mark the whole room as complete. There is also a Decluttered Rooms Checklist worksheet at the end of the chapter, as well as additional printable copies in *The Clutter Fix* bonus at HomeMadeLovely.com/tcfbonus, so you can do this purge as often as needed and still have checklists to use as you go!

Let's dive right in!

☐ Declutter the Front Porch

Your entryway extends to your porch. It's one of the first things anyone sees when they arrive at your house, including you. So, give it a quick clean-up if things have accumulated that don't belong there. Look after these:

☐ Dirty doormats
☐ Empty/old plant pots
☐ Recycle or garbage bins
☐ Garden tools
☐ Wreaths

Put away the obvious items, toss any trash, and straighten up things like mats and chairs. Maybe sweep and hang a new wreath, just for a little extra curb appeal. Repeat seasonally. (See chapter 14 for seasonal decluttering instructions and checklists.)

Woohoo! You've decluttered a lovely welcome to your home!

☐ Declutter the Entryway

Entryways often become a dumping ground for everything—keys, junk mail, shoes, coats, purses, sunglasses, sunscreen, and more. Entries are also the first place you see after enter-ing your home, so it pays big dividends in your sanity to have the entryway clutter free. That's why we tackled the entryway back in the 10-Day Decluttering Short-cut. If you didn't do that, now is the time to declutter this high-traffic space. Even if your entryway is pretty small, you'll still likely have a significant amount to declutter. Work through the list, one area at a time. Repeat seasonally, or as needed.

> **A decluttered home matters because**
>
> "It creates energy and an environment in which my creativity can thrive."

☐ *Shoes and Boots*

Go through all the boots and shoes. Toss any that are beyond worn out. Kids are notorious for growing out of shoes quickly, leaving mom-mas exhausted from all the excess pairs. So, if you have kids, go through their boots and shoes with them. That way they can try each pair on. Donate any that don't fit.

☐ *Chairs and Benches*

Next, clear off the benches or chairs in the entry. Much like chairs in master bedrooms, chairs and benches in entryways tend to be a clutter catch-all spot. Whether it's an unused jacket, old newspapers waiting to go out for recycling, or kids' backpacks, the entry chair or bench is not the place to leave those things long-term. Figure out what needs to be tossed or recycled; put away anything else. Then set up routines (in chapter 14) so that there's no excuse for the seating in your entryway to become a dumping ground again in the future.

☐ *Tabletops*

Entry tables are also a magnet for all kinds of clutter. Which makes sense given their location. But with a little planning, they can be helpful and organized.

Remove everything that doesn't belong on the table and then grab a pretty bowl for keys and loose change. If paper clutter seems to accumulate on your front hall table, maybe even grab a tray to collect it in and then add looking after that to your paper decluttering routine.

☐ *Coats and Jackets*

Along with shoes, jackets can become messy in the foyer very easily. Especially if you live in a part of the country that experiences the distinct weather of all four seasons. I know our entry gets very cluttered in the spring because we are wearing winter coats for early morning dog walks, but only need a light jacket at midday.

Go through all the jackets and coats to make sure each one fits its owner. Put any that don't fit any longer into the donate box. Revisit coats and jackets seasonally to avoid too much clutter in the coat closet.

☐ *Mats and Rugs*

Entry mats generally need cleaning and not decluttering. But if you change out your mats for the seasons, now is a good time to make sure any currently unused mats are put away and the ones you're using are clean and tidy. This only takes a few minutes but makes a big difference in the look and feel of your entry.

☐ *Seasonal Gear*

Again, if you live in a four-season climate like I do, you will likely have off-season gear in your entry at any given time. After sorting through it and removing unneeded items, make room in the entry closet to store what you are keeping, or find room somewhere else in your home for it. Then at the start of each season, switch out all that paraphernalia for the current season.

☐ *Key Hooks*

This one should be a quick declutter. Take all the keys off the key hooks. If any are for locks you no longer use or own, toss them. Then put the keys you need back on the hooks. One trick I love for keys is to use my label maker and create a label for the key ring that says what it's for.

Wahoo! Your entryway is clean and clutter-free!

☐ Declutter the Dining Room

How cluttered your dining room is depends on where it is in your house (specifically in relation to an outside door), how many purposes it serves (home office, homeschool room, crafts space), and how much storage space you have in it currently. Repeat these steps to declutter the dining room as needed or a couple of times a year.

☐ *Dining Room Table*

If your table has become a dumping ground for all the papers and other things, this is the most logical place to start.

First, put away anything that you can immediately see that has an existing home in the dining room or elsewhere in the house.

Then, sort like with like into piles:

- Kids' artwork
- Bills
- Craft projects or supplies
- Puzzles and games
- Books
- Laptops and cords
- Anything else that has accumulated on the table

Throw out or recycle anything that can be tossed. Put things you're going to donate into your donate box or bag; ditto with things you want to sell into the sell pile, box, or bag.

Next, determine where to store the remaining items.

For example, if crafts, games, and puzzles are done in your dining room regularly, that's totally fine. But you need to come up with a storage solution for them. Maybe a basket on the sideboard, or a drawer or two in the hutch, depending on your family's Organizing Personalities. *The dining room tabletop is not the place to keep those things when you're not actively using them.*

Finally, after all is put away, wipe down the dining room table.

☐ *Dining Room Hutch and/or Buffet*

Other common clutter magnets in the dining room are drawers and cabinets of buffets and hutches and their surfaces.

Follow the same procedure for any buffet and hutch surfaces as you did for the dining room table.

Then empty one drawer or cabinet section at a time and sort like with like:

- Napkins and napkin rings
- Placemats
- Chargers
- Candles and candlesticks
- Table runners
- Tablecloths
- Serving dishes
- Anything else that has accumulated

If anything is broken beyond repair, trash it or recycle it if it's recyclable. Then put any pieces you don't want or use anymore into your donate box.

Finally, return each category of item to the cabinet or drawer in a logical fashion, so that things are easy to access and use. Add or use bins, baskets, and drawer organization as appropriate for your family's Organizing Personalities.

Wipe all the buffet and hutch surfaces to remove any dust and debris from your cleaning. Sweep the floor, and you're done!

Look at you go! You're the proud owner of a nice, tidy dining room!

☐ Declutter the Living/Family Room

If you have both a living room and a family room, work through only one at a time. Then repeat the steps for the other room. And repeat seasonally as needed.

☐ *Hotspots and Surfaces*

Often living rooms and family rooms end up with items that truly don't belong there, due to daily use and traffic. So, the best place to start decluttering these rooms is to remove anything that belongs in another room. Grab a basket or box and do a quick once-through for these things. Set the box aside until you're finished decluttering the room.

☐ *Wash Fabrics*

Run a laundry load or two to wash all the pillow covers, slipcovers, and blankets from the living room and family room. Check the washing instructions just in case. I always buy machine-washable throw pillow covers and throw blankets because we really live in our living room, and those things need frequent washing.

☐ *Drawers, Cabinets, Surfaces*

Pull everything remaining out of drawers and off surfaces. Sort like with like:

- Toys
- Dog toys
- DVDs
- CDs
- Blankets and throw pillows
- Remotes
- Video games
- Video game controllers
- Anything else specific to you and your family that has accumulated

Now, throw out anything that is irreparable.

Put any items you don't use or no longer need into the donate bin.

Take stock of what's left and determine whether you need more storage containers or storage furniture. Add baskets for frequently used items like throw blankets or pet toys. Replace a plain ottoman with a storage ottoman if you need more space. Use a dresser as a pretty side table in the living room that doubles as DVD storage. Put everything away in a logical and organized place. Just keep your family's Organizing Personalities in mind and choose storage pieces accordingly.

☐ *Decor*

Next, take a look around at your decor. Is it possible that you have too much going on that is causing visual clutter? Have you put up more and more art over time and now have a mishmash of random things? Do you have too many tchotchkes on surfaces? Think about eliminating anything you don't *love* to help create a more visually clutter-free space, then get rid of it.

☐ *Cords*

Now, manage those cords. Try to use cords that are the right length for the space and purpose. Don't use a twenty-foot cord when a ten-foot cord will do. Tuck cords safely behind furniture if possible. This will still keep them out of sight, without too much effort. When hiding them that way isn't possible, make them as straight and as neat and tidy as possible, and zip-tie them together in place. Or get a cord channel that can be painted to match the walls or baseboards to further disguise clutter from cords and cables.

☐ *Finishing Up*

Replace the freshly washed and dried throw pillow covers and slipcovers.

Then take the keep box that's filled with things that belong in other rooms, and return them to their proper spaces.

Woot! Your living/family room is all done and looking fine! Take some time to enjoy the new clutter-free space! You deserve it.

☐ Declutter the Kitchen

There's almost nothing as nice as coming downstairs in the morning to a clean kitchen. It's so satisfying to know you're not starting your day with a mess. But kitchens tend to appear cluttered quickly due to daily use and lots of necessary items. However, if you divide your kitchen into zones, you can greatly minimize this clutter, regardless of your Organizing Personality. Near the stove, there should be pots and pans storage and a spot on the counter or in a nearby, easy-to-access drawer for cooking utensils. Unless you bake daily, put your baking dishes, baking supplies, and small appliances farther away from the everyday prep area. Storage containers should have their own zone, probably near the plastic wrap and freezer bags. We have a garbage/recycling/food-waste zone near our sink, which is opposite the food-prep area, which is beside the stove. Zones make kitchen organization so much easier! Repeat these steps seasonally as needed.

☐ *Countertops and Sink*

Take a look at your counters. Put away the things that don't need to be out on display.

Kitchen Clutter Tip: If it doesn't live on the counter, put it away! In other words, it doesn't need to be on the counter if it doesn't get daily use.

If you find you don't use something and want to get rid of it, and it still functions well, start a pile on the counter in an out-of-the-way area. We'll add to that donate pile when we declutter the rest of the kitchen. Now wipe down and rinse the sink for some extra visual satisfaction.

> **A decluttered home matters because**
>
> "Being able to find things quickly instead of wasting time would be less tiring."

☐ *Cabinets*

Chances are you have a couple of cupboards that contain similar things. Open and empty one or two related cupboards at a time. For example, we have two drawers that contain our plastic reusable food containers. So, I'd empty and sort those at the same time because things could go back in either drawer depending on how they fit.

Once you've emptied everything out and decided what stays and what goes, clean out the cabinets really well with a cloth or a vacuum. Then put items away logically.

☐ *Drawers*

If you didn't do the 10-Day Decluttering Shortcut, or if your junk drawer has gotten away from you again, start with the junk drawer and empty everything out. Sort. Get rid of duplicates, like that extra can opener.

Also get rid of kitchen tools that don't serve more than one purpose, like a melon baller or an avocado slicer. The exception is if you literally use that one-purpose tool daily and it truly makes your regular life easier.

If you keep things just because someone once told you that a kitchen "should" have them, but you never use them, they end up cluttering your space and your mind!

Return the keepers to the drawers in an organized, logical fashion. Repeat for each and every drawer in the kitchen.

☐ *Fridge and Freezer*

Have a garbage bag and food waste bag for compost handy. Also, have on hand some all-purpose spray cleaner and a reusable cloth or paper towels for wiping down the shelves inside the fridge and freezer. (In the kitchen I tend to use a washable cloth for cleaning most surfaces, simply rinsing as it gets dirty. But sometimes I find the fridge and freezer's smooth surfaces need paper towels because the reusable cloth just pushes the bits and crumbs around, while a paper towel grabs them a little better. Use whatever you prefer.)

Begin in the fridge and remove everything one shelf at a time, starting with the top shelf, working your way down. Check dates on packaged foods. Toss anything that is past its "best before" date or that looks or smells funky. Work your way across each shelf and then move to the one underneath that, and so on, tossing and sorting as you go. I tend to put things that need to be tossed in one spot on the counter as I go. That way I can batch my steps. For example, I'm working in the fridge going through everything all at once. I'm wiping each shelf as I go and putting things that are good back in an orderly fashion. Then when I'm finished going through all the shelves and door buckets, I toss what needs tossing into the food waste/compost and rinse any containers and load them into the dishwasher. I try to be responsible by taking produce out of plastic baggies and putting it in the food waste/compost while putting just the plastic baggie in the garbage. The same goes for jars and other recyclable containers. I empty them into the compost bin and then rinse the jars before putting them in the recycling bin.

After you've done the fridge, move on to the freezer portion of your fridge, using the same process.

Finally, sweep the floors to clean up any crumbs that have spilled from your cleaning.

☐ *Extra Freezer*

If you have a chest or upright freezer in your basement, mudroom, or garage, you will need to set aside a bit of time to go through it as well. To do this, it helps to have a table nearby to set everything on as you clean and sort.

First take everything out, one package at a time. Toss anything that is beyond use, such as freezer-burnt meat or veggies. Then sort like with like:

- Meat, by type
- Veggies
- Fruit

- Freezies/popsicles/ice cream/other desserts
- Bread
- Butter and cheese (if you're freezing these)
- Prepared meals like soups, chilis, casseroles

If any packaging looks like it needs reinforcing, now is a great time to add another Ziploc or wrap it in another layer of plastic wrap. Touch up any labels that may have smudged. And put everything back in an orderly fashion.

If you need to get some storage containers for the freezer, make sure you measure your available space and make note of what needs organizing. Grab *The Clutter Fix* bonus at HomeMadeLovely.com/tcf-bonus for a printable you can use to sketch your storage plan onto. I like to use plastic-coated wire baskets and clear plastic buckets. Typically, I find that storage bins designed for holding things in the office (like files) work just as well as those specifically designed for freezer storage—and they're usually much cheaper to buy too! Repeat this clean out at least seasonally or as needed.

Look at you go! Now your freezer is organized too!

☐ *Pantry or Other Nonperishable Food Storage*

If you're fortunate enough to have a pantry, it's likely that it gets cluttered from time to time. Which makes sense, since food items are rotated through it very frequently—especially if you have teenagers or young adults living at home. If you don't have a traditional pantry, you probably have a few cupboards that you use for storing your nonperishables. Declutter those now following these pantry decluttering instructions.

To begin, quickly go through everything while it's still in the pantry and toss anything that has expired or is past its "best before" date.

Next, do a quick once-through the pantry again and grab anything your family no longer eats (due to new dislikes or food sensitivities) and put those items into a donation box.

Now you can pull out items from the pantry one type at a time for sorting.

Take out all the canned goods and sort them on the counter into types:

- Each type of veggie
- Each type of fruit
- Meats and fish
- Beans

Then do the same for the boxed and other packaged goods:

- Crackers by type
- Pasta by type
- Popcorn, chips, and other snacks by type
- Nuts and granola bars
- Cereals and oatmeal
- Condiments
- Salad dressings
- Salsa and spaghetti sauce
- Jams, nut butters, and spreads
- Pickles and olives
- Spices and seasonings
- Oils and vinegars
- Everything else

Once you have everything pulled out and sorted, wipe down the pantry shelves, cans, and packages if needed. Then put everything back in, sorted by type. You can use baskets and bins and can sorters if you wish, based on your Organizing Personality.

And voilà! Now you have a clean and clutter-free kitchen!

☐ Declutter the Bathroom

Even the smallest bathroom has several zones that act like clutter magnets. Here's how to clean out the bathroom clutter from every size and type of washroom. Repeat annually.

☐ *Shower and/or Bathtub*

If you have one, remove the shower curtain and wash and dry it.

Take a quick inventory and get rid of any empty bottles and containers in the shower. Same with any dull or rusty razors.

Remove the rest of the bottles and containers to the counter for sorting. Combine any shampoos or other things that can be combined to reduce the number of bottles you will need to put back in the shower.

If you have bath toys, take them all out and toss any damaged or moldy ones. Then clean the keepers by soaking them in vinegar and water or running them through the dishwasher.

Lift the bath mat and give the shower and/or tub a good cleaning. Clear the drain of any hair and debris (ack!) and rinse everything well. Cleaning technically isn't necessary when decluttering, but you might as well do it while you're at it. Then use a basket or mesh toy bag to corral any tub toys in the bathtub area.

Now return the sorted bottles and necessities to the shower. Keep things like razors up and out of reach of young children. Rehang the clean and dry shower curtain and replace the bath mat.

Bonus Tip: Add hooks to the wall or an over-the-shower hook if you find you're hanging towels over the shower curtain rail or the shower door. Get an extra shelf or caddy for the shower if bottles and things are cluttering up the floor.

☐ **Bathroom Cabinets**

Bathroom cabinets can become messy really quickly, and it's no fun to be searching for the hair gel when you're late for work. Out of sight, out of mind seems to be the prevailing attitude toward bathroom cabinets, at least at our house. (Please don't judge me by my kids' bathroom!)

But bathroom cabinets can easily be organized and decluttered. Much like the kitchen, you're going to want to go through one drawer or section of the cabinet at a time. The exception to this is if you have one big cabinet that isn't divided inside, which you would do all at once.

To start, take everything out of the cabinet or drawer. Immediately toss anything that is expired, and recycle empty containers. Then sort like with like:

- Shampoo and conditioner
- Soaps
- Razors
- Medicines
- Feminine hygiene products
- Toilet paper
- Hair dyes
- Hair products
- Nail care
- Hair dryers and curlers
- Tooth care
- Everything else

After tossing the easy stuff, for each category determine if you're going to use it, or if it's something old you no longer love. Toss anything you're not planning to use again or are keeping just in case. If you have new, useful toiletries you simply won't use, check your local shelter to see if they could use them rather than throwing them out, or see if a friend wants them.

Before you put things back, give the cabinet and drawers a quick wipe and then figure out how best to store things based on how you use the bathroom space and your family's Organizing Personalities.

For example, in our master bathroom, one top drawer has all my makeup in it because I use it almost every day and it's easy to access; another drawer has toothbrushes and toothpaste in separate trays—one for Dean and one for me. Then the lower cabinet contents including extra soap and toothpaste are organized into clear, labeled plastic bins (to protect the contents from any potential water leaks from the sink above), stacked neatly behind closed cupboard doors. Things like toilet paper and feminine hygiene are in the cabinet right next to the toilet, and razors and shampoo are on the side nearest the shower—in case those items are needed while we're using the loo or taking a shower!

Be ruthless in your purging here. You don't need that bottle of shampoo that made your head break out. But you could probably use the extra tube of toothpaste from the brand you've used religiously for the last decade. Think logically and purge accordingly. Then assign new homes so that everything is quickly and easily accessible and tidied up after each use.

☐ *Bathroom Counters*

Bathroom counters can easily become the dumping ground for all the bathroom things. Especially with multiple people sharing the space. But if you assign all the necessary bathroom things a home, it will be much easier to keep the surfaces neat and tidy.

Take stock of what's on your counters. If certain things do need to live on the countertop, like the hair spray or face wash, corralling them in a wipe-able, splash-proof tray is one of my favorite hacks for bathroom organization. Put away anything that doesn't need to be on the counter. Give the counters and sink a wipe and rinse.

Yay, you! Your bathroom is all tidy! Repeat for each bathroom in your house.

☐ Declutter the Bedroom

In addition to the list of supplies at the beginning of this chapter, to declutter the bedroom you'll need a mirror (for trying things on), a duster (for surfaces), and a sticky roller (for clothes). Again, no matter how small your bedroom is, it can still be divided into zones for cleaning it out as follows. Repeat the steps below for each bedroom in the house, then repeat them seasonally as needed.

☐ *Dresser*

If you have more than one dresser, purge only one at a time. Open each drawer, one at a time, and take everything out. Toss anything so worn out that it can't be donated. Put anything you know you don't wear into a box or bag for donations. Try on everything that remains. If something doesn't fit well, and/or doesn't make you feel 110% awesome . . . get rid of it.

The same goes for those clothes you're holding on to that you're hoping to fit into again someday. If you haven't worn them in over a year, it's time to get rid of them. (Unless you are or have been pregnant, then give your body another year to adjust before purging your prebaby clothes.) The physical space they're taking up is causing you unnecessary stress. But the emotional stress they're causing is even worse. I know personally, every time I glanced at my smaller clothes, thoughts rolled through my brain like *I should be doing so much better with my diet*, or *I should be exercising way more*, or *Why am I not back into those clothes yet?* And then I'd proceed to mentally beat myself up for not doing better. I don't need that kind of negativity in my life! When I finally bagged up and got rid of clothes that I'd moved to this house in a box several years ago, I felt so much better and accepting of where I was. Of course, that doesn't mean I don't want to try to do better with my diet and exercise, but I don't need those clothes randomly shaming me every time I walk by them. Do yourself a favor like I did and just get rid of them!

> **A decluttered home matters because**
>
> "As a person who suffers from anxiety when my house is messy or full of clutter, I feel the anxiety more and find it hard to relax in my own home because all I see is stuff everywhere."

☐ *Closet*

In the closet, go through all your clothes and shoes and bags and hats and whatever else you keep in there.

To do this, sort through one category of clothing at a time. For example, go through all your blouses/tops first. Toss or recycle anything that is beyond repair and then put the shirts you no longer *love* into the donate box. Then try on what's left to make sure it fits well. Only put back the tops and blouses that you love and that fit well, hanging first the sleeveless tops, then the short-sleeved tops, and finally the long-sleeved tops in a neat row. Or if you prefer, hang them by color.

Repeat this same process of toss, donate, try on, and hang up for each type of clothing in your closet:

- Blouses
- Sweaters
- Jackets
- Skirts

- Dresses
- Long sweaters
- Casual shoes
- Sandals

- Boots
- Dress shirts
- Suits
- Everything else

Remember, your old clothes that are in good condition could really be a help to someone else, so don't hold on to them *just in case*. Instead, be a lovely blessing by passing them on.

☐ *Nightstand(s)*

Nightstands have a way of collecting all sorts of clutter. Things like books you've already finished, ticket stubs, Chapstick, cough drops, hand cream, photos, chargers, receipts, reading glasses, notes, and more.

To purge your nightstand, empty one drawer or cabinet section at a time. Immediately throw out any garbage, such as wrappers or clothing tags. Also, toss any receipts that are no longer needed. While they were good to hold on to for a little while, you don't have to keep all of them forever. Like that Christmas gift receipt that you hastily shoved into the bottom drawer while you were wrapping that last gift on Christmas Eve. It can likely be thrown out now. (The same goes for old receipts you've stashed elsewhere in your house too.)

Then, sort what's left, like with like—photos with photos, notes with notes, etc.

If you don't have a designated place for storing memorabilia like photos, ticket stubs, and notes, consider putting a basket or small box in your nightstand or closet for them.

Return any unused chargers and books that you're not currently reading to their proper homes. Place often-used items like your Chapstick and hand cream in the top drawer where they're easily accessible. Then clear off the nightstand surface, putting things away where they belong, and give it a good dusting.

Tip: If you wear prescription glasses, it's a good idea to hold on to one extra old pair, just in case. But if your nightstand has accumulated more than one spare pair (see that, I rhymed!), it's time to donate them to someone who needs them. You can ask your optometrist where the best place is to drop them off.

☐ *Hotspots*

Finally, in the bedrooms, there always seems to be those hotspots that collect random things too. Clothes tossed over a chair, dresser surfaces scattered with things that need to be put away, etc. Now is the time to return those items to their proper homes and do a quick dusting and vacuuming, for good measure.

In kids' rooms, have them help you with the same tidying and decluttering process. With smaller kids (and even teenagers who get overwhelmed or distracted easily), give them one small chore at a time so they don't feel quite so overwhelmed by the task. Things like "pull everything out from under your bed," "gather all the socks from the floor," or "find all the hair ties and clips on the dresser and put them away." That way, you're not doing all the work, and they're learning to take better care of their things by returning them to their proper places.

Yippee! You've decluttered another room!

☐ **Declutter the Linen Closet**

Because things are constantly put into and pulled out of linen closets by numerous people in a household (much like the pantry), they quickly become a cluttered jumble of sheets and towels. Follow the steps below to declutter your linen closet (or wherever you keep towels and bedding if you don't have a linen closet), and repeat seasonally.

Just like other spaces, in order to create a clutter-free linen closet, you need to pull everything out of it and sort through it. Any sheets, towels, duvets, or pillowcases that are irreparably stained or worn should go in the trash or be cut up to use as rags (but only if you genuinely need rags). Others that don't fit any current beds or color schemes in your home should go into the donation box. Someone else is sure to be happy to use them if they're in great condition.

Then, sort like with like again:

- Facecloths
- Hand towels
- Bath towels
- Bath mats

- Beach towels (if applicable)
- Duvets
- Quilts

- Blankets
- Bed skirts
- Shams
- Sheet sets

Sheet sets can be sorted and organized by complete sheet sets (fitted sheet, flat sheet, and pillowcase) or you can fold and stack all the flat sheets together, all the fitted sheets together, and all the pillowcases together. It depends on how you use them and how your family best finds them and puts them away.

Once you've folded and sorted everything, you can either create nice, neat piles on the closet shelves or get some pretty labeled baskets and stack each type of linen inside the baskets on the shelves. Eventually, I'd love the basket method, but for now, with the kids at home, that would be too "out of sight, out of mind" for them, so we have orderly piles. Well, they're orderly *most of the time*.

Congrats! You just decluttered your linen closet, formerly one of the messiest spots in the house!

☐ Declutter the Laundry Room

Laundry rooms come in all shapes, sizes, and locations in a house, so what you keep in yours may be different than what we keep in ours. But typical laundry rooms contain the following:

- Laundry supplies like soap, dryer sheets, fabric softener, stain remover
- Other household cleaning supplies like bleach, window cleaner, floor cleaner, polishes, extra dish soap, hand soap
- Light bulbs and batteries

- Vacuums, brooms, mops
- Ironing board and iron

To declutter your laundry room, take everything out of cabinets or off the shelves. As we decluttered our laundry room, we needed to bring everything into the nearby dining room, because our laundry room is too small to move in when things are out of place.

Toss or recycle anything that is empty or broken beyond repair.

Sort and decant laundry soap into pretty containers to help your laundry space be more aesthetically pleasing.

Place baskets strategically in the room if laundry goes straight into the laundry room at your house. Otherwise, keep floors clear to leave room for baskets that are brought in from other rooms. We keep one small basket in the corner of the laundry room for tea towels, dish-cloths, and the main floor's powder room towels. Otherwise, our tiny laundry room floor space stays clear.

Try not to store anything on top of your washing machine and dryer. If you're short on space, it's okay to put the laundry soap and dryer sheets there if absolutely necessary. Otherwise, it just becomes a messy dumping ground.

Organize any shelves or cabinets by putting like with like, and use pretty, labeled containers whenever possible, according to the Organizing Personalities in your house.

Yippee! Your laundry room is all sorted!

☐ Declutter the Playroom

Playrooms (and sometimes family rooms or bedrooms where toys are) can get cluttered super-fast. Kids just have this way of taking out every toy in sight and not putting anything away. But their playroom or play space doesn't have to be overwhelming. In fact, cleaning it out can be the catalyst for major changes in your home.

Kids become overstimulated very easily. And while we think a play space chock-full of toys will keep them occupied for hours, the opposite can be true as they get overwhelmed by too much stuff.

To clear the clutter from the playroom or play space, grab your donate box (and sell box if you're selling items). If there is any organization currently in the space, work in each zone, one section at a time. If, however, the playroom is a big free-for-all space, work through the whole space a little at a time.

First, collect any garbage and broken toys that can't be repaired. Place those into a trash bag.

Then remove any toys that your kids have outgrown and that are in good shape, and place those in your donate box. Sometimes it's best to do this *with* your kiddos, especially if they get attached to things and have a hard time parting with their belongings. (Remember the story about my daughter's little blue elephant?)

Now sort everything that is left, like with like. That means all the trains, dolls, books, cars and trucks, etc., with the same category of toys. If, after you've sorted the toys into piles, there are duplicates or unnecessary multiples of some toys, add those to the donate box.

The steps you've taken so far in the playroom should have narrowed down the toy collection a fair amount. But if you find that you still have too many toys—either too many for the space, too many for the number of kids you have, or too many that you're worried you'll still be cleaning up all the time—make some choices about what you can pass along to other people. Put those into the donate box.

Now decide how you will store the toys you are keeping. Will it be in one big toy box (I don't usually recommend this) or in individual bins by type of toy (my favorite)? Remember to keep it easy, though, with simple storage you can show your kids how to use, rather than having to put things away for them.

What We Did with Toys When Our Kids Were Little

When our kids were little, the best way we found to organize their toys was to have open bins (no lids) on shelves, at their eye level or below, that were less than half full. When they were too young to read, I took pictures of the toys that belonged inside each bin and attached the photo to the front of the corresponding bin. Once they got older and could read, we labeled each bin with what went inside. That way, even if a bin got entirely dumped out, everyone knew what belonged inside it and it didn't take long to clean up.

Each day, before lunch, before dinner, and finally before bedtime, we collectively tidied up the kids' play space with a "Ten-Second Tidy" like in the kids' show *The Big Comfy Couch* that was on TV when my kids were little. By enforcing these practices and habits, their play space *almost* never got completely out of hand. I recommend the same sort of routine for your playroom too. (More on routines for clutter-free maintenance in chapter 14.)

Repeat in any rooms where the toys live at your house.

Wahoo! The playroom is clutter-free!

☐ Declutter the Home Office

Oh, the home office! I've worked at home for years now. But many North Americans experienced working from home for the first time in 2020, while at the same time learning firsthand how hard it can be to keep a home office tidy and clutter-free (among a myriad of other 2020/2021 life lessons). "You may think you're not bothered by your overstuffed filing cabinets or the stacks of paper on your desk. But scientists at the Princeton University Neuroscience Institute have used fMRI and other approaches to show that our brains like order, and that constant visual reminders of disorganization drain our cognitive resources and reduce our ability to focus. They also found that when participants cleared clutter from their work environment, they were better able to focus and process information, and their productivity increased."[1]

> **"Have nothing in your houses that you do not know to be useful, or believe to be beautiful."**
> —WILLIAM MORRIS

Thankfully, it's fairly simple to declutter a home office and reduce the unnecessary burden of stress that can come from a messy office.

Repeat the steps below as needed, such as after a major work project or before you go on vacation. *If any of the items below are not part of a separate home office, use this time to declutter and organize the space where they do live in your home, like your dining room or a spare bedroom.*

☐ *Desktop*

In order to make any real progress in the office, you need to sort and declutter your desktop first. A decluttered desk is partly practical—it allows you ample space to work—and partly aesthetic. Much like a bed that is made makes a bedroom appear neater, a desk that is cleared off makes an office look much neater too.

Begin by tossing any obvious trash in the garbage. Then go through and sort like with like—papers, pens, dishes, whatever is sitting on your desk. Then put things away where they belong. We'll tackle the other individual office things one at a time.

☐ *Papers*

Most clutter in a home office is related to paper: mail, invoices, bills, and all manner of paper piles. If you have piles of paper randomly stacked everywhere in your office, now is the time to sort through them, one by one.

First, toss any junk mail, expired coupons, or fliers into the recycling bin.

Keep and file any receipts you need for tax purposes into appropriately labeled file folders in your filing cabinet. Check your local tax laws for how long you need to keep paperwork related to income taxes, and shred anything that's older than that.

If you get duplicates of bills both electronically and by mail, shred any paper copies that are sitting in your piles. If you have the option and haven't yet take advantage of it, make a note in your schedule to sign up for electronic billing once you've cleared the clutter in your office to help reduce the papers that come into your home.

Add a paper tray or two to your desk to collect papers that you need to deal with, such as bills before they're paid or other correspondence that needs your attention. Make it a priority in your schedule to empty the paper trays each week.

☐ *Filing Cabinets*

If you have filing cabinets, you know that they can easily become a monstrosity over time. To declutter yours, go through it now and then set up a time to go through it again once a year just before tax season to purge unnecessary paperwork.

First go through the file folders and pull out any records that are old and don't need to be kept any longer. Generally speaking, you need to keep tax-related documents for seven years (in case of an audit). But check online or with your local tax office to be sure. These you will want to shred, so do that now or set aside a pile and make sure to schedule a time to do it.

Then make sure that the remaining file folders are labeled correctly and in the correct order within the cabinet. The simplest way to organize files is alphabetically, but you could use another system (like organizing by finances, medical, personal, and business) if you'd like.

Finally, go through each folder to make sure it only contains necessary items and nothing extraneous or old. Be sure to shred any documents that have personal info on them, and then return the "keep" files and folders back to the filing cabinet.

☐ *Bookshelves*

Bookshelves in an office (or anywhere in the home) can also become messy and disorganized over time.

To purge yours, sort through each shelf one at a time, and set aside any books you no longer need.

Sort the remaining books on the shelves. You can sort them by color (pretty but not necessarily wise if you're not used to finding books that way), author, subject, or title.

Wipe the shelves as you go to remove dust that has surely accumulated.

When you're done, either donate the books you no longer want, sell them, or trash them (if they're in complete disrepair).

☐ *Office Supplies*

Most homes have office supplies even if there isn't a home office: things like stamps, paper, pens, tape, and markers. The steps for sorting these items are much the same as sorting a junk or other kitchen drawer.

To begin, empty everything out and sort all the office supplies from wherever you keep them.

Get rid of duplicates, like that extra stapler or hole punch. Also get rid of things you don't ever use. If you keep things just because someone once told you that you should have them, but you never use them, they end up cluttering your space and your mind!

Finally, return the keepers to the drawers or cabinets in an organized, logical fashion using the organization method that suits your Organizing Personality. For example, if you're a Nothing Out + Simple Organizer, make sure you have drawer or cupboard space that you can toss your pens into easily when you're tidying up at the end of your workday. Or if you're an Everything Out + Detailed Organizer, make sure you have several clear mason jars sitting on a shelf or on your desk for the different types of pens, markers, and highlighters that you use.

☐ *Tame the Cords and Label Them*

The other mess that tends to make a home office space look and feel cluttered is cords from many electronic devices, like computers and printers.

Review your cord situation and make sure things are plugged into the closest and most logical outlet. Using a label maker or even just a marker and masking or washi tape, label each cord near the plug end so you know what it's for at a glance.

Then straighten the cords as much as possible into neat bundles. Tuck any that you can behind furniture to visually declutter the space.

Tie cords together with zip ties when possible to keep them neat and tidy.

Now do a quick dusting and vacuuming and you're done! A neat and tidy home office is finally yours!

☐ Declutter the Basement and Attic Storage Areas

Basements and attics are typically used for the storage of memorabilia and seasonal items, like Christmas decor and lights. But they are often cluttered and contribute to the feeling that the house is a mess, even when you can't see them. When you're cleaning these spaces out, you should set aside a decent amount of time and enlist help if you'll be needing to move large things or many boxes—especially if your basement or attic has been a family storage space for decades! Repeat the steps below either seasonally or as needed annually.

☐ *Set Up and Use Zones*

When decluttering your basement or attic storage spaces, declutter in zones.

What I mean by that is to work in sections:

- Shelves
- Bins and boxes
- Big stuff like furniture

Work on only one at a time—for example, the shelves—and finish sorting each zone before moving on to the next. Otherwise, you'll end up with an even more overwhelming mess.

As you work through sorting your zones, put things into either the toss, donate, or keep pile. If you have a lot of items, use multiple boxes for each or simply put items in one of two piles ("keep" or "get rid of").

As soon as you are done with each zone, move the donate boxes to the car and schedule time to drop them off. Put trash immediately into the trash.

Now choose how you will reorganize the items you are keeping. Here's where you'd sort things "like with like." Old mementos can be stored in a less accessible location in your basement or attic, while you'll want to keep things like seasonal decor more accessible. Keep Christmas lights with other Christmas lights. Sort your ornaments and tree decor by color, so that you can easily access just the ones you want next year.

Make sure you label everything well! You can use a simple permanent marker on a cardboard box or even on a Rubbermaid tote. Or you can print labels from your printer or a label maker. Just make sure to be clear and accurate when labeling to avoid having to haul all the boxes out to find that one little thing you need.

Once you've completed all the steps for one zone, move on to the next, and repeat until your attic or basement is clutter free and organized.

Hip-hip-hooray! Your basement and attic are all sorted and decluttered!

☐ Declutter the Garage

Garages are where so many necessary and unnecessary things gather in a home. Apparently, "twenty-five percent of people with a two-car garage are unable to park their cars in it because of the amount of 'stuff' being stored."[2] Old kids' toys, half-finished projects, sports equipment, car parts, seasonal tools, and more find their way to the garage. As a result, garages are often one giant clutter hotspot to be avoided at all costs. We have friends (who shall remain nameless) who are wonderful planners and utterly amazing people. But they are teased in good fun by other friends (who will also remain nameless) for their messy garage. And Dean and I are great at keeping our home organized and clutter-free, and yet we have struggled to keep the garage tidy in the past. It's sort of like a kitchen pantry or freezer in that things are always coming and going, so it's hard to keep on top of. This has always been true for us, especially for the first couple of years after we move to a new house (we've moved a lot), when we don't yet have any organization specific to that garage in place. Once we do a big clean out—or a few—and get some storage in place for the necessities like car-maintenance supplies, kids' toys, and tools, it's so much easier to do a quick tidy up when we need to work on a project or park the van inside during a snowstorm.

You will want to plan your garage decluttering for a weekend that is due to have great weather since you'll be pulling so much out of the garage and decluttering with the door open. Also, try to plan your garage purge for a time when you can get to the dump and donation centers immediately after you finish to get rid of all your unneeded stuff, so it doesn't stick around.

Keep in mind that if the garage is "hubby's space," there may be some negotiating and back and forth about what stays and what goes, and about where things will live in the garage when you're organizing. Repeat the following steps seasonally as needed.

If at all possible, pull everything out of your garage to start with. I know this can be tough, but it is the best method for clearing out garage clutter. If you can't do this, work through one area at a time and try to clear the floor space of large items so you have room to work.

Immediately throw out bits of garbage and add empty recyclable containers to your recycling bins. Of course, if any of the empty containers had paint or other household chemicals in them, you must dispose of these properly. If you have any of this household hazardous waste, gather it in one spot until you can get it all disposed of safely. But be sure to do so as soon as possible.

Next, if you haven't used any garden or sports equipment for two years, put those into your donate box or pile.

Sometimes if an item is in good shape and we simply don't need it anymore, we will put it at the end of the driveway with a "free" sign taped to it. Often, a neighbor will pick it up and say it was just what they needed. Of course, if it doesn't get picked up within a day or so, we donate it or otherwise dispose of it.

Make sure you don't have any duplicates of tools or equipment that you don't need. At our house, we keep three snow shovels, because the kids help with snow shoveling, and having only one shovel led them to argue over who had used the shovel the longest and whose turn it was. But if only one of you shovels, you only need one. The same goes for other duplicate things. Donate what you don't need anymore or haven't used for a year or two.

Now you need to sort the remaining items, like with like. Sort all the sports equipment together, the yard tools, the tools, camping gear, etc.

A great tip for keeping garages clutter-free is to rent instead of buy the things you will only use once a year or less: things like large power tools or golf clubs. Better yet, borrow them for free from a friend or neighbor. Just remember to give them back in the same or better condition than they were in before you borrowed them.

Next, assign everything a space in the garage. This step will very likely require the purchase of additional organizational tools like bins or shelves and pegboards. Make note of the size of things and the size and shape of your garage. Create a master sketch on a piece of paper if that helps you. Then purchase what's needed. Obviously, if you've pulled everything out of the garage, you will need to put it in the garage while you go buy the storage and organization pieces. Just be sure to keep like with like. And don't get caught up doing other things until you completely finish the job and your "keep" items all have a home.

This garage clean out may take more than one weekend if your garage has gotten way out of hand. And you will likely need to purge and shift things around in the garage seasonally and as you need access to things like camping gear, snow shovels, or outdoor Christmas lights and decor.

Give the floor a good sweeping and go celebrate! Your garage is finally clean!

☐ Declutter the Paper

Okay, paper clutter is technically not a room, and we did tackle some of it in the 10-Day Decluttering Shortcut, as well as in the kitchen and home office. But it can be a tricky thing to sort through and get a handle on. So, in addition to sharing how to deal with it previously, I'm sharing how to declutter your paper piles here too. That way if you're specifically setting time aside to work on paper messes, you can just flip to this section and get to work.

If you have a paper pile sitting around, as most people do, here's how to tackle it:

- Go through the paper pile and sort it into three piles—bills, junk mail, and other (birthday cards, family letters, etc.).
- Focusing on the bills pile, go through and sort the papers by the billing company. If you've ignored this for a while, you may have a lot of sorting to do. Then stack them all together. For example, because I run a business from home, I keep all the utility bills together for tax purposes. Sort your pile however you need to for your home.
- Now hop on your computer with your sorted bills stacked in front of you, go through the pile, and sign up for each company's digital/online billing as you go. Choose to use an email address whose inbox the bills won't get lost in.
- Now, file the paper bills that need keeping (for tax purposes or reference), and shred and toss those you don't need to keep. If you don't have a filing system set up yet, sort your bills into labeled file folders and put them somewhere safe for now.

Going forward, when each bill arrives in your inbox, you can either

- Open it and pay it immediately, or
- Favorite/star the email and add the amount owing to your ongoing budget spreadsheet, and then pay it when the time comes to do your banking each month. Once it's been paid you can file the email in a bills, utilities, or other appropriate folder in your email program.

Next:

- Sort the junk mail into pure junk mail (unsolicited flyers and coupons) and catalogs.
- If you've marked any pages in the catalogs of items you want or things you want to remember, take a photo of those pages with your phone. Then move those into their own folder or album on your phone so you can find them easily when needed versus scrolling through all your phone photos.
- Now go online and unsubscribe from any catalogs or companies that you opted in to receive mail from. You can do this piece by piece individually, or you can Google how to unsubscribe from junk mail using a bulk unsubscribe service.
- Add a note to your physical mailbox that says, "No fliers" or "No junk mail." Etsy has some pretty decals for this if you'd like something more attractive. You could also make your own with a cutting machine like a Cricut or Silhouette. This works for community mailboxes too if you put a note inside your individual locked box.
- Now take that pile of junk mail and catalogs and recycle it!

If any junk mail does make its way into your house after this, make sure to check that your "no junk mail" note is still in place and simply toss the offending paper into the recycling bin immediately. Commit to not letting it sit around in a pile anymore!

Then go through the other pile and decide what needs keeping and where you will keep it. For instance, will all birthday and Christmas cards be kept, or just the ones with a personal note in them? Where will they live? In a filing cabinet, or in a box with other memorabilia? Make decisions, recycle what you don't want, and put away the rest.

Yippee! You've made huge progress getting existing paper clutter out of your home! We'll talk a bit more about organizing and managing paper in chapter 14.

☐ Declutter Your Inbox

Oh, the email inbox and all those little unread notifications—aka one of the major stressors of the modern era. While email does make our lives easier, and we can connect with others much more quickly than in the past, it can also get way out of hand really quickly. Decluttering your inbox is a bit like decluttering the paper in your house: you need to tackle what's there, and then you need to prevent more email clutter from coming in.

If your work or personal inbox is chaotic, the first thing you need to do is scroll through the first one or two "pages" and see if there's anything urgent. That will normally be about twenty-five to fifty

> **A decluttered home matters because**
>
> "I feel happy when my home is clean and organized; therefore, I can think more clearly and put more effort toward being a wife, mom, and homeschool teacher. My home needs to be a safe haven!"

emails or so, depending on your settings. If it's any further back than about fifty emails, it's likely that the urgency has—ahem—*passed*. Address anything that needs your immediate attention—like it's a matter of life or death that you respond right now. Otherwise mark them as important and come back to them when you're done decluttering. Then select all your emails and mark them as read. Yup, just, go ahead and clear those unread notifications. Take a big deep breath and enjoy that for a second.

Then scroll through the first page or two of your inbox and mark any emails as spam that you know you didn't subscribe to. After you've done that, feel free to bulk delete any emails from that sender.

Now, scroll through and select several emails at once by sender/ category. For example, if you have Amazon and you've done a lot of ordering lately, scroll through and select all the Amazon emails on the first page. Then file them in a folder called Amazon Orders. Repeat for other categories or senders.

Your goal is to get your inbox to a totally manageable place. Some call it inbox zero. You want only things left in your inbox that are pending or that still need your attention. As soon as you've dealt with something, it should be filed in a folder. Try to keep on top of this daily or at the very least weekly. I never quite get my inbox to zero emails, but I do keep it to about twenty-five (or quite often less) during the week and a little more on the weekend (because I don't file them on the weekends).

☐ Declutter Your Computer

I recently got a new laptop and as such had to declutter my iMac to get the files all duplicated and organized. It was a big job even though I'm generally pretty good with filing my digital files. But man, did it ever feel good to get it done! Like a huge weight was lifted that I didn't even realize was there.

First, go through each major folder in your computer—pictures, documents, and downloads are common folders to find on any computer—and delete duplicates, obvious trash, and anything you know that you know that you know you don't need. Empty the trash or recycling bin on your computer.

Then begin to sort the keepers into appropriate folders and sub-folders. I tend to store my files like this: Year → General Category → Specific Category → Item. Take our taxes for example. They would be filed in folders like this: 2021 → Finances → Taxes → Income Taxes. Then each individual file and document would be inside the Income Taxes folder—our returns, receipts, statement of accounts, and so on. Repeat for everything on your computer. Treat yourself to a fancy drink or fun snack, or schedule this out over a few days if you need a little motivational help to get this task done. (Repetitive tasks like this are not at all my favorite.)

Bonus Tips: I highly recommend storing your files "on the cloud" (and not just your hard drive) with a service like Google Drive, Dropbox, or iCloud. I personally like and use Google Drive because it's drag and drop and easy to use and share with family and business team members. But be sure to read the terms and conditions of any cloud service you use to be sure you're comfortable with them and the security your chosen cloud has. In addition, it's good to keep a digital copy of important files on an external hard drive and paper copies of extra important things like life insurance in a fireproof, waterproof safe too. I also highly recommend a backup service like Backblaze for backing up your computer and other devices regularly. These extra tips may or may not help you to be more organized, but they definitely fall under the "peace of mind" category.

☐ Declutter Your Other Devices/Phones

Another thing that makes life easier are our phones, tablets, and other similar devices. But they too can become unwieldy with too many apps. To purge your phone, take a look through every one of your apps to see if you're using them. If you're not using one, offload or delete it entirely. If there are apps that you can put together in a folder—say all your banking or social media apps—do that to streamline the look of your screen. Then go through your pictures and videos and delete all the duplicates, fuzzy pictures of the floor, and the extra ninety-nine photos of baby or Fluffy that you don't need. Finally, update any remaining apps that have updates pending. In all honesty, I'm terrible at keeping my apps up to date and often pass my phone to one of my kids, who is naturally good at administration and organization, and have her do it while I make lunch or something. Repeat these steps as needed.

Make sure to get *The Clutter Fix* bonus at HomeMadeLovely.com /tcfbonus for examples of different types of organizing systems in each room for each Organizing Personality.

Decluttered Rooms Checklist

As you work on decluttering each room in your home, use this checklist to mark off spaces when they're finished. You got this, girl!

☐ **Porch**
- ○ Dirty doormats
- ○ Empty/old plant pots
- ○ Recycle or garbage bins
- ○ Garden tools
- ○ Wreaths

☐ **Entry**
- ○ Shoes and boots
- ○ Chairs and benches
- ○ Tabletops
- ○ Coats and jackets
- ○ Mats and rugs
- ○ Seasonal gear
- ○ Key hooks

☐ **Dining Room**
- ○ Dining room table
- ○ Dining room hutch and/or buffet

☐ **Living Room**
- ○ Hotspots and surfaces
- ○ Fabrics
- ○ Drawers, cabinets, surfaces
- ○ Decor
- ○ Cords

☐ **Family Room**
- ○ Hotspots and surfaces
- ○ Fabrics
- ○ Drawers, Cabinets, Surfaces
- ○ Decor
- ○ Cords

☐ **Kitchen**
- ○ Countertops and sink
- ○ Cabinets
- ○ Drawers
- ○ Fridge and freezer
- ○ Extra freezer
- ○ Pantry or other nonperishable food storage

☐ **Bathroom 1**
- ○ Shower and/or bathtub
- ○ Cabinets
- ○ Counters

☐ **Bathroom 2**
- ○ Shower and/or bathtub
- ○ Cabinets
- ○ Counters

☐ **Bathroom 3**
- ○ Shower and/or bathtub
- ○ Cabinets
- ○ Counters

☐ **Master Bedroom**
- ○ Dressers
- ○ Closets
- ○ Nightstands
- ○ Other furniture

☐ **Bedroom 1**
- ○ Dressers
- ○ Closets
- ○ Nightstands
- ○ Other furniture

☐ **Bedroom 2**
- ○ Dressers
- ○ Closets
- ○ Nightstands
- ○ Other furniture

☐ **Bedroom 3**
- ○ Dressers
- ○ Closets
- ○ Nightstands
- ○ Other furniture

☐ **Bedroom 4**
- ○ Dressers
- ○ Closets
- ○ Nightstands
- ○ Other furniture

☐ **Guest Bedroom**
- ○ Dressers
- ○ Closets
- ○ Nightstands
- ○ Other furniture

☐ **Linen Closet**

☐ **Laundry Room**

☐ **Playroom**

☐ **Home Office**
- ○ Desktop
- ○ Papers
- ○ Filing cabinets
- ○ Bookshelves
- ○ Office supplies/desk drawers
- ○ Tame the cords and label them

☐ **Basement/Attic Storage**

☐ **Garage**

☐ **Other Paper Clutter**

☐ **Your Inbox**

☐ **Your Computer**

☐ **Other Devices/ Phones**

Decluttered Rooms Coloring Page

Color in each room as you declutter it!

PART 4

MASTER MAINTENANCE MODE

CHAPTER 13

Please Don't Start Here!

ka a warning about getting ahead of yourself.
If you're jumping ahead to this part hoping that habits and routines will fix your clutter issue, but you haven't decluttered anything or done any of the mindset work yet, stop!

Obviously, any positive routine or habit you implement can only help you. Like brushing your teeth more often can only be good for you. Or reading five pages a day of a good book will have you reading several new books a year. But if you haven't decluttered and gotten the excess stuff out of your house before adding the decluttering routines, you will find yourself frustrated with a lack of serious progress. Sort of like if you were to brush your teeth and then go and drink a cup of coffee and eat a donut. Your teeth wouldn't stay clean very long. You need to do the decluttering purge first and get your mind in the right place *before* you create habitual routines in Maintenance Mode.

So, if you've skipped ahead, back you go, lovely. Do the decluttering and mindset work first. Then come back here for Maintenance Mode.

Got it? Good!

CHAPTER 14

Routines and the Awesome Power of Habits

At the beginning of this book, I mentioned that there were three main overarching parts to a lovely, clutter-free home (aside from the quick wins in part 1). The first is to get your mind in line with your home goals. The second is to do a big purge of your whole home, one room at a time. And finally, the third is what we're going to work on now: keeping the clutter out. I like to call it Maintenance Mode.

In Maintenance Mode, you've already completed the big decluttering process. You've purged and gotten rid of all the excess, the duplicates, the things you don't need anymore or no longer have the space for. You feel lighter. You and your home can finally breathe without the pressing weight of all the clutter. And you've created, or at least determined, the best organizing systems for you and your family according to your Organizing Personalities. But now you may be wondering, *How do I hold on to that clutter-free home? How do I KEEP it that way?* Maybe, like many of us, you've decluttered before, and not too long after, your home was full of stuff again, and then you felt defeated, frustrated, and overwhelmed. You were back to square one. If you've ever had this happen, you are definitely not alone. Many of us mistakenly assume that if we could just purge the clutter once, we'd never have to think about it again. However, while we hopefully never let our homes become a complete disaster again, we will still need to maintain our spaces and purge and reorganize certain parts of our homes seasonally (or at other regular intervals). We do this by creating routines and habits.

What Are Routines and Habits?

Routines *are small actions that you add to various parts of your day little by little until they become ingrained* habits *you no longer have to think about doing. You just do them automatically, or routinely.*

Much like clutter, habits don't happen overnight. They happen incrementally. You probably already have many routines that you do on autopilot. Activities like brushing your teeth before bed or turning the coffee pot on when you wake up. You didn't always do those things. You developed those habits over time—either on purpose (your parents made you brush your teeth every single day until it was just automatic) or by accident (you needed caffeine in the morning after a rough night and the coffeepot was your way to that glorious first cuppa).

Habits can be really good. But "**there are two kinds of habits: those that serve you, and those that don't.**"[1] If your house is a cluttered mess (or was before you began reading this book), at least some of the habits you've developed in your home—very likely without even realizing it—are not serving you, are they? Habits like leaving the living room a mess before bed and waking up frustrated because you left it that way again. Or piling the dishes in the sink until everything is stinky and attracting flies. Or never putting things away when you're done with them and then tripping on them for days or weeks afterward. Those are habits. They're just not good ones.

James Clear says, "There are all sorts of myths about how long it takes to build a new habit: 21 days, 30 days, 66 days. The truth is, there is nothing about time passing that magically forms a habit. ***Habits are created based on repetition and frequency, not by the clock ticking.***"[2] This goes hand in hand with what Jeff Olson talks about in *The Slight Edge*, that each day, each moment even, you are moving away from or toward the person you want to be. James Clear also says, "Every action you take is a vote for the type of person you wish to become."[3] If you choose to eat French fries and a cheeseburger for lunch one day, no biggie, right? Tasty fun food is another one of the many joys in life. But what if you chose to do that every single day? Or what if you decided not to read your Bible, just today? You're tired and you need the extra sleep. But if you do that for 365 days in a row, you won't have read any Scripture for an entire year. Or what if you didn't go for that walk today? That's okay, right? But again, if you chose to do that for months on end, you won't have gotten any exercise in far too long. Seemingly small decisions add up over time.

> **A decluttered home matters because**
>
> "I spend a lot of time at home, and I want to be comfortable in my space and not have it evoke feelings of shame, guilt, or aversion by it being cluttered or unsightly."

The same principles apply in your home. *Each day you're moving away from or toward the home you want to have.* It doesn't really seem to matter if one day you don't pick up the toys or load the dishwasher. You can always do it tomorrow. And that's totally okay from time to time, when someone is sick, or there are some other extenuating circumstances. But what happens when tomorrow turns into the next day, and the next, and you repeatedly avoid tidying up? That's when you end up with a disaster in your home and bad habits that can be tough to break.

So, what do you do if you're already stuck in this rut? If you've developed bad habits with regard to clutter and messes in your home? Well, one of the best ways to build a new habit is to identify a current habit you already do and then stack your new behavior on top. James

Clear refers to this as habit stacking.[4] Rather than pairing your new habit with a particular time and location (which can be tricky with young kids at home or shifting schedules), you pair it with a current habit. Because of how our brains work, our current habits are already built into our brains. They've been strengthened over years. So, using them as a trigger for new habits is easier than just randomly adding new ones. This is how you create good routines. Based on this, the habit stacking formula is as follows:

"After/Before [CURRENT HABIT], I will [NEW HABIT]."[5]

You can use this formula for developing all sorts of habits in your life. But I'm going to encourage you here to use it for your home habits. For example:

- After I finish dinner, I will load my dishes into the dishwasher. (And I will show the kids how and remind them to do the same.)
- After I get out of bed in the morning, I will make my bed.
- After I pour my cup of coffee each morning, I will empty the dishwasher.
- Before I go to bed, I will tidy the living room.
- Before the kids go down for a nap, I will show them how to tidy the playroom.

"Once you have mastered this basic habit stacking structure, you can begin to create larger stacks by chaining small habits together. This allows you to take advantage of the natural momentum that comes from one behavior leading into the next."[6]

For example, your morning home habit stack—or routine—could look like this:

- After I get out of bed in the morning, I will make my bed.
- After I make the bed in the morning, I will turn on the coffee machine.
- After I turn on the coffee machine, I will empty the dishwasher.

Or your evening home routine could look like this:

- After I finish dinner, I will put my dishes in the dishwasher.
- After I put my dishes in the dishwasher, I will make the lunches for tomorrow.
- After I make the lunches for tomorrow, I will wipe down the counters.

And so on.

I highly recommend that you add *one to three new things* to your day at a time until they happen like clockwork, rather than needing mental effort to remember to do them. For example, if laundry is your nemesis, make sure you set a laundry habit stacking routine and stick to it almost religiously until you don't have to think about it so much anymore. Or if the kitchen often seems out of hand, make sure you implement an evening and morning routine that serves you well in this area and stick to them until they are mainly just habit each day. Then you can add new routines in other areas of your house where needed over a bit of time. Use the worksheets at the end of the chapter to write down which new things you will add to your day to make into habits and routines.

Another helpful trick to making habits stick is to make them as easy as possible by setting up zones for tasks. In my kitchen, for example, the paper towels are near the stove and the cutting board, where I do all my food prep. This simple "zone" organization means that when I inevitably have food waste when preparing food, I'm in the habit of grabbing a paper towel to collect it on, which makes it super easy to pick up and toss into the compost rather than having a huge cooking mess when I'm finished. Make your home, stuff, and routines work *for* you, instead of against you!

Okay, so we've talked about habits and routines and how they will help you immensely in keeping your home clutter-free. Now I'm going to show you the routines I use in my home and how *you* can set up routines that will become habits in *your* home that will serve *you* best.

My habits and routines may not work for the stage you are at with kiddos at home or for your schedule, since it's likely different than mine. I know that my routines now are definitely different with teenagers and young adults in high school and college than they were when my kids were little and the bulk of the homeschooling was on my shoulders. Look at what chores and house stuff should become routine, and see how I do things on the next few pages. Then use the worksheets at the end of the chapter to plan out what will work best for *you*.

Daily and Weekly Routines

There are a few routines that will benefit you greatly in your home and keep it looking and feeling wonderfully clutter-free. Some of these routines will be daily routines; some will be weekly. Some will occur much less frequently, like the seasonal routines we'll talk about toward the end of the chapter.

Here are the routines that we have incorporated at our house that I think are the most helpful:

- Morning Routine
- Lunchtime Routine
- Evening Routine
- Weekly Routines

And here are some of the chores that we include in those routines.

1. Dishes

If you hand-wash your dishes, make it a habit to wash them quickly after every meal and snack. If you use a dishwasher, make sure you're rinsing and loading your dishes as you are finished using them. Then as soon as the dishwasher is full, run it. Empty it as soon as it's finished running, or at the next logical point in your day.

At our house, keeping up with the dishes is a bit of a moving target. Since Dean and the kids share the dishwasher duties, and some are more diligent than others with their chores, some days are better than others for dishes. Ideally, though, the dishwasher is emptied in the morning. Then everyone rinses and loads what they use, as they use it, into the dishwasher during the day. When the dishwasher is full, we run it. Honestly, I have to do quite a lot of reminding. But I *remind* and rarely *do* for anyone. Eventually, all three kids (some sooner than others) will live on their own and need to keep up with their own dishes themselves, so I look at these daily reminders as teaching moments rather than nagging (although it does sometimes *feel* like nagging).

2. Tidying Up

As you go about your day at home, tidying as you go is a fabulous habit that will serve you well. Fix the pillows on the couch when you get up; put the remotes and books away when you're finished; hang up coats when you come in the door. Just don't procrastinate and leave these seemingly little things until "later," because they will pile up.

At our house, we tidy up based on anchor points in the day. This is pretty much habit stacking. For example, before I make lunch, I straighten the throw pillows in the living room (I like the living room to be tidy), load any of my own dishes into the dishwasher from breakfast, and wipe up any leftover breakfast mess. Then I make lunch. Before I go up to get ready for bed, we make sure the living room is once again straightened and that the kitchen is tidy.

3. Snacks and Mealtime Cleanup

Much like washing dishes and loading and unloading the dishwasher needs to become a routine, you need to simply clean up after each meal. Rinse the pots and pans, wipe down the table and counters, and sweep under the table. This will keep these chores from sitting there taunting you.

At our house, as I previously mentioned, everyone is supposed to load their things into the dishwasher after each snack and meal. And Dean and I work together after dinner to clean the kitchen, with him loading the dishwasher and washing any big items and me wiping down counters and the table.

4. Cleaning

If you do a little bit of cleaning each day, you may not dread the tasks so much. Maybe assign one day to sweep floors and another to dust, etc. Or break up the house and give everyone a section to clean weekly. Or leave yourself ten to fifteen minutes at a certain point in your day (like immediately after your coffee, or as soon as your kids go down for a nap) and choose a cleaning chore that seems to most need doing. One day perhaps it's sweeping the floors, another maybe it's spot-cleaning the bathroom. Adding cleaning to your regular routines helps to keep the house from becoming a filthy mess.

At our house, everyone has assigned chores throughout the house: sweeping, toilets, counters, dusting, etc. Most cleaning chores are done weekly or every couple of weeks. But I tend to wipe down the main floor's powder room sink and counter and change the hand towel every couple of days since that bathroom gets the most use. I also swap out the kitchen dishcloth and hand towels daily. And I run the Dyson stick vac when I notice dust or dog hair wafting around because it only takes a few minutes. Most of these things I do right after my breakfast, before I sit down to work.

5. Meal Planning and Shopping

Meal planning can be your best friend when it comes to keeping unnecessary food clutter out of the house, plus it saves time. If you meal plan, you know exactly what you need and won't buy extra useless items that will just go bad and need your maintenance. I have lots of meal-planning ideas and resources on the blog. Make sure you check them out if you need help with this.

At our house, I do all the meal planning, and Dean and I share the grocery-shopping responsibilities. I've always meal planned, at least to some extent, to keep a handle on our grocery bills. But I've found that if I meal plan consistently, using my Capsule Pantry method, kitchen food clutter is kept to a minimum. (You can find out more about this on the blog too, homemadelovely.com/capsule-kitchen.)

6. Laundry

Laundry is one of those ongoing tasks that can really cause a lot of stress-inducing clutter in a home. But if you purge your closets and make sure you only keep what you need and use, there will be less to wash overall. And although you may have to throw in a load more often—like if you have only ten pairs of underpants instead of fifty—you won't have such massive piles taunting you when you do the laundry. And if you do one load—wash, dry, fold, and put away—a day, the laundry will seem less overwhelming than if you leave all the loads for the entire household for one day.

There are a few ways to handle laundry well:

1. If you're home during the day, or for several hours in the evenings, add laundry to your *daily* routine. Generally, start a load in the morning, move it to the dryer at lunch, and then fold and put it away in the evening. If you are consistent, this should work to get all the household laundry done most weeks.

2. If you are not home during the day, you could do one full load—wash, dry, fold, and put away—each evening.

3. Or you could do several loads from start to finish on the weekends, if this is the only time available. This method can feel more overwhelming, though, to keep on top of. So only use it if there's no other option.

Choose whichever method and schedule that will work for you for the laundry so that you're getting each load fully finished—including folded and put away. If one method doesn't work, try another. Laundry isn't fun for most people, honestly. But it's a necessity, so you need to find a solution.

At our house, this is a case of do as I say and not as I do because— *shocker!*—I don't do the laundry, aside from the occasional load. Dean took over doing the laundry when the kids were little because I'm not so good at production-type work (my creative brain has a hard time with repetitive tasks), and he is more particular about how things like laundry are done, so it was just best for our marriage that he took over the laundry. (Here's where I'd insert a winky face emoji, if emojis were included in books!) And the kids have done their own laundry since they were seven, nine, and eleven respectively. They each have an assigned day of the week, with a buffer day between for those kiddos who tend to be a little slow getting their laundry done, to avoid bickering about whose laundry is still in the machines. So, laundry doesn't normally figure into my own routines now. But it did—or was supposed to—when the kids were younger.

7. Paper Organization

Now that you've decluttered your paper piles, keeping your papers in check will be about the system you set up and your routines. As for filing systems, there are myriad ways to go about this and each one will work differently, depending on your Organizing Personality. Some people prefer to go entirely digital, scanning everything into an online filing system, while others still use traditional hanging files and filing cabinets. And as I mentioned before, some people (Detailed Oragnizers) do well with many subcategories of file folders (separately for individual stocks, mutual funds, gas, electricity, and water bills), while others (Simple Organizers) do better with larger, more broad categories (one folder each for all investments, utilities, bills). Choose a system and try it to see if it works for you. If you find a winner on the first try, awesome! If not, just try a different paper-organization method until you find one that you can maintain with ease. I know there's one out there that will work for you!

At our house, what works best for us is a combination. We get some bills by email and others by snail mail. We keep our paper sorted in three overarching ways:

1. Short-term papers like this year's bills, receipts for recent purchases, and bank statements go in a small hanging file unit tucked in the kitchen drawer next to the desk area. The hanging folders have files with general filing categories, like "utilities," and one each for the kids for the current year where we put things as soon as we receive them.

2. Longer-term papers like tax receipts and warranties go in the filing cabinet in the basement, as do each previous year's paperwork (like tax returns and the kids' files) that needs keeping.

3. Papers that need keeping indefinitely like insurance policies, wills, passports, marriage certificates, etc., all go in a locked and waterproof firebox for safekeeping and are only handled when necessary.

You can adopt a similar system or choose something entirely different. Just don't put this off, or your paper piles may take over again!

8. Making Your Bed

Making your bed each day doesn't technically reduce the clutter in your home, so this is optional. But it does reduce the *visual* clutter you see every time you walk into your bedroom.

At our house, the bedmaking tends to vary by person. We have a couple of kiddos whose beds are rarely made and one whose bed is always made. And I sometimes make our bed and sometimes not, depending on the day and how busy I am—and how likely I am to go back upstairs and be annoyed by an unmade bed. When we lived in our other houses, a bungalow and a back split, I made the bed more often because I saw our bedroom more often during the day.

Okay, so now that you've been introduced to the types of things to include in your routines, keep reading to learn about specific routines that I use and also check the end of the chapter for worksheets that will help you to create your very own handy routines that will easily become habitual.

Our Morning Routine

Setting morning routines that become automatic is necessary because they help us to get a few important things done on autopilot first thing. Your morning routine may look different than mine, depending on whether you work from home like I do or leave your house for the day, and also if your kids are home or off to school each morning. Here is what our morning routine looks like as far as house stuff goes:

- Dean gets up before anyone else to leave for work, makes coffee (usually French press), and some mornings empties the dishwasher too.
- I get up awhile later and pour myself the coffee that Dean has left for me or maybe a cup of tea. While it's reheating, I go around and open the curtains, put yesterday's dish towel and dishcloth in the laundry basket in the laundry room, and take out new ones.
- I try to remember to take any meat we may need out of the freezer to thaw for dinner at this point, but sometimes I forget and don't do it until lunchtime. I definitely need to take my own advice and make this into a habit, tied to finishing my coffee in the morning or something.
- I drink my coffee or tea while I do devotions and the kids get their own breakfast. Then I grab something quick to eat and start my workday.

The kids have been getting their own breakfast on weekdays for a while now. I know lots of homeschooling moms whose kids get their own lunch, but we have lunch together. This is just how it works for us at our house. You can obviously do what works for you. Use the worksheets at the end of the chapter to create your own morning routine.

Our Lunchtime Routine

I tend to run on the side of workaholic a little, which means it's hard for me to shut off to take a lunch break. But my kiddos need the touchpoint in the middle of the day, and I frankly need the pause too. When it's time for lunch we turn on the TV to signal to all of us that it's lunchtime. I know it sounds weird, but the kids and I (especially the girls and I while my son is at school or working) always watch one episode of a familiar series like *Star Trek TNG* or *Gilmore Girls* at lunch. Then:

- We make lunch. Often I will do this, but there are plenty of times that one or all of the kids will help too.
- We clean as we go, loading the dishwasher and wiping counters.
- After we eat lunch, we rinse our dishes and load them into the dishwasher. Often, by this point, the dishwasher is full again and I turn it on before we head back to work and schoolwork for the afternoon.

Use the worksheets at the end of this chapter to create your own lunchtime routine.

Our Evening Routine

I believe the evening routine is one of the most important routines of all because the state you leave the house in before you go to bed will make a huge difference in how your day starts out in the morning.

And we all know how awful it is to wake up to a dirty, messy kitchen with a sink full of dishes. Our evening routine looks like this:

- Prep and cook dinner, putting things into the sink or dishwasher, disposing of any trash, recycling, or food waste, and wiping countertops as we go so that there's less mess after dinner. This is where my paper towel for food waste comes in handy.
- When we're finished eating dinner, each person is responsible for clearing their own dishes into the dishwasher and composting their own food waste into the under-counter food waste bins (already lined with compostable bags for easy disposal on garbage day).
- The kids help to put away any condiments we've used with dinner.
- Dean loads any remaining dishes into the dishwasher, while I wipe down the table and counters as they are cleared.
- Often there are dishes leftover in the sink, so Dean will also likely empty the dishwasher again before bed, and I will spray and rinse the sink at that time too.
- When we're ready for bed, I pick up the dog toys (he spreads them around more than a toddler does with their toys!), fluff and straighten the living room throw pillows, and put the TV remotes away while Dean takes the dog out and the kids get themselves ready for bed.

Our kids are now teenagers and young adults, but they've been helping set and clear the table since they were much younger. I actually kept them using plastic dishes for a long time so that they could clear their spots safely.

If you've read our daily routines carefully, you may have noticed that we run the dishwasher a lot—usually two and sometimes three times a day. There are five of us, currently two to four of us who are home all day, eating a full three meals plus snacks. The ones not here all day have lunch containers that need washing. We also run many of our pots and pans through the dishwasher too, so they take up a lot of space.

Use the worksheets at the end of the chapter to set up your own evening routine.

Our Weekly Routines

There are other things that need looking after in a house that don't happen daily, but that best happen on a weekly basis. Things like grocery shopping and meal planning and budgets and bills. You may wonder why I'm bringing them up (more than once, even) in a book about clutter and organizing your home. But if your grocery shopping and meal planning are not made into a routine and accounted for in your home, they can contribute to kitchen clutter. And if you don't get your budget and bills set up in a routine and make that habit, the paper clutter will once again take over. So, planning for them and making them into habits by habit stacking will help immensely to keep the clutter from coming back into your home.

At our house, I look after the budgets, bills, banking, meal planning, and grocery shopping in one day, on Fridays. I like to call these "Finance Fridays" because all of those things involve our finances (groceries are a huge expense around here). I start by recording business income, then I move on to checking the bank accounts, updating the budget, and paying bills for our household and our business. If I've handled any paper bills or statements, I put them in their appropriate files when I'm finished. Then I either update the current meal plan or create a new one and make the grocery list. Depending on how the week has gone and what else is happening, I will then either order groceries to be delivered or plan an in-store grocery shopping trip for that

> ## "Holding on to clutter is not like having money in the bank. It's not currency."
>
> —KRISTA LOCKWOOD
> (Motherhood Simplified
> Facebook Group)

afternoon or another time that works. When the groceries arrive (either by delivery or by Dean and I going shopping) *everyone* helps to put them away.

Seasonal Routines

Seasonal routines are ones that happen—well, obviously—seasonally. They are natural times to do some bigger tidying and decluttering jobs around the house. Much like yard work at certain times of year—overseeding the lawn in the fall and spring, shoveling in the winter, or adding mulch and soil to the gardens in the spring—these seasonal touch points will help to keep things inside and outside your home humming along smoothly. Keep in mind that seasonal decluttering is technically different from seasonal cleaning, although you can clean as you go about decluttering if you'd like since it's a natural time to do so. But I want you to focus on the actual decluttering here. Specifically, so that your home is easier to maintain and clean for the rest of each season.

How to Implement Seasonal Routines

In order to fit seasonal decluttering into your life, and make it routine, you should schedule it and give yourself a deadline. Look ahead in your calendar to see when you have an available weekend or a couple of partial weekends. Or look at a week when you can spend ten to twenty minutes a day every day for several days in a row, with a timer to get the job done. If you want to make these seasonal decluttering sessions into habits that happen with the change of season, and you should, tie them to other things like the first day of spring, summer, fall, or winter, or to the weeks before Easter or Thanksgiving. This is sort of like habit stacking but linked to seasonal events rather than more frequent daily or weekly habits. Then, of course, you need to add decluttering to those days in your schedule. Use the seasonal checklists at the end of this chapter as you get things cleaned up in and around the house each season. *You can get additional printable copies of the Seasonal Decluttering checklists with* The Clutter Fix *bonus here: HomeMadeLovely.com/tcfbonus.*

Note: You may notice that there is some overlap with each season. For example, I include decluttering outdoor toys at the start of both summer and fall. That is deliberate because in one season you're preparing to use the toys and in the next you're tidying up and putting them away for a while. If you're just starting to implement seasonal routines, you will definitely need this overlap each season, at least until you go through a full cycle of seasonal decluttering. But once you get in the groove and habit of these seasonal decluttering sessions, you may not need to go through things quite so thoroughly that second time. At that point I recommend going through things at the end of each season before storing them away to avoid storing and organizing clutter unnecessarily.

At the Start of Every Season

If you live somewhere with four distinct seasons and the climates to go with them, you should take one to two hours at or just before the start of every season to clean out clothing and accessories that no longer fit or work for you and for your family. To do this, tackle one closet and dresser at a time, starting with the oldest person in the house and moving down to the youngest.

- Empty each closet and dresser out as you did during the purge phase and sort like with like.
- Put clothing items that are in good shape but no longer fit into a donate bag or box, and toss things that are irreparable into the trash.
- Pass on any hand-me-downs that will work for your younger children as you sort the clothes.
- Also, as you go about cleaning out dressers and closets seasonally, keep a pen and paper or your phone handy to jot down what each person needs for the season, including sizes. That way, when it's time to buy new things, you will know exactly

what is needed and avoid buying duplicates or having to re-visit those drawers and closets again.

The same should be done for each season's sports equipment for everyone in your family. Depending on sports and activities that you, your children, and your spouse are involved in, you should:

- Go through the previous and current seasons' equipment to check for wear and tear and also for sizes. For example, in the spring, go through the hockey gear from winter and then check on the soccer equipment for spring.
- Purge the things that are broken or don't fit anymore.
- Make a list of anything that needs buying or sourcing as you go, so it's easier when the time comes to get those things.

I'm including decluttering clothing, outerwear, and sports equipment as well as food storage again as part of each season's checklist so that it's easier to remember at a glance what to declutter each season. Use the checklists at the end of the chapter each season as you declutter. Don't forget to get yourself some extra printable copies of the checklists at HomeMadeLovely.com/tcfbonus.

Decluttering around Major Events

Sometimes it's not only the day-to-day or even the change of seasons that upsets the delicate balance of a decluttered home and lifestyle, but rather the major events and celebrations in our lives. Birthdays, Christmas, moving, and having a baby all come with their own excitement, mess, and sense of change. Decluttering before and/or after these events is super important to keeping Maintenance Mode humming along . . . and for keeping the clutter out of the house!

After Christmas or a big birthday celebration, evaluate any gifts and set aside those that need to be returned, donated, or regifted. Just as we discussed in chapter 7, you can talk with family and friends about your new clutter-free lifestyle, and if they're open to it, give them suggestions for gifts that are wanted and needed that suit you and your family's stage right now. I definitely recommend that you do this. Honesty is the best policy for everyone.

Birthdays and other special celebrations are also a great time to revisit what you currently have in the house that's taking up space and time (maintaining it, tidying it up, or cleaning around it); perhaps do a mini purge *before* such events. This is a bit like a preemptive purge to make room for what you know is coming. You can also do the same type of mini purge after a celebration. The key is to do it very shortly afterward so that you don't become overwhelmed by the clutter and give up on your clutter-free home goals, just because you left things too long. To do this type of mini purge, follow the same steps as you would for a full purge, focused only on the spaces affected, like the birthday boy or girl's bedroom:

> **A decluttered home matters because**
>
> "It just makes me happy to walk in and not see a cluttered mess everywhere I look. I have four kids, and it can sometimes be hectic and I need to be able to find things quickly."

- Pull everything out
- Sort like with like
- Donate, toss, or sell whatever you aren't keeping
- Assign a home for what you are keeping

You can go back to chapter 9 to review and follow the steps there for decluttering and organizing any space, or you can visit chapter 12 and follow the specific steps for the room you want to declutter. This preemptive clearing out should really help avoid a lot of clutter overwhelm around these wonderful celebrations.

Other major life changes like moving, changing jobs, or having a baby are also good times and reasons to purge unnecessary clutter from your home and life. For example, before moving you will definitely want to do a clutter sweep of your entire home. There's no reason to expend the time and energy to pack things you don't need. What a waste! Follow the steps in chapter 12 for each room to do this again. Then after you move, if you find that you haven't opened a box or missed those things that are still packed away after a year, get rid of it without even opening it. You obviously don't need it.

Try to plan ahead for what you know will be potential clutter-inducing events, and you will find them much less overwhelming.

Two Helpful Maintenance Mode Hacks

So even if you purge all the things and set up great organizing systems, you may find certain areas of your home still get messy easily. That's why looking at them seasonally as we discussed is a good idea. There are also a few more simple hacks that I want to share with you that will help you in maintaining your clutter-free home.

The Donate Box

The Donate Box is something that is crazy-handy to keep clutter at bay. It can be a box or a basket or even a garbage bag if you like. The overall idea of it is to keep a specific spot in your home ready to accept donated items year-round.

At our house, for the longest time, one corner of our upstairs hallway was accidentally designated as "the donate spot." When one of the kids would outgrow something or simply be done with it, they would always ask me where they should put it. And I just defaulted to saying, "The upstairs hallway corner."

Well, this inevitably spread out across the hall and became a tripping hazard. Now we keep a tote in the same corner that is labeled "Donate." Once the tote is full, the contents get emptied into a garbage bag, and it gets taken to the van to be donated the next time someone is driving by Value Village (our closest donation spot). This is a super easy hack to keep the "Donate" clutter contained and controlled.

The Memorabilia, Finished Art, and Finished School Work Boxes

For years we've also kept memorabilia boxes for each of our kids in their bedroom closets. They have no lids and are labeled so that the kids know what they're for and can easily add things to them. That way when they have a camp T-shirt or a special memento from a trip that they want to keep, rather than cluttering up their dressers or desks, it goes into the memorabilia box. When a box gets full, we take a bit of time to go through it and decide with them what they really want to keep. If we eliminate enough so the box is no longer stuffed full, we just put it back up in the closet for use for a while longer. If the box is indeed full, we close it up and store it in the furnace room and get them a new labeled box to put in their closet for more memorabilia. Fortunately, even at this point we only have a couple of boxes for each kid stored away because we take the time to make sure it's all stuff they genuinely want.

We used to do the same thing back when arts and crafts were a daily occurrence at our house, with separate boxes for each of the kids' finished arts and crafts and their finished homeschool work. For a while, we just piled these things in a cupboard. But that quickly got out of hand. So, we implemented the separate boxes idea, and it worked really well. The boxes were easily accessible for the kids on a shelf. When they were full, we'd sort through them and decide what to keep and what to recycle and then start fresh with new boxes when needed.

Add these small box hacks to your home, and they should really help keep clutter to a minimum.

Setting Up Your Routines Prep Work

1. What home things do you need to get done every single day (i.e., dishes, tidy living room, pick up toys)?

2. What times of day are best for the daily chores you listed above? Write down each chore and the time of day that will work best for you for handling it.

3. What things need to get done every week (i.e., x loads of laundry, cleaning the bathrooms)?

4. What days are best for each weekly chore you listed above? Write the chores you listed above and then jot down the best day or time to do them.

5. What chore(s) causes the most stress around the house that could be reduced by creating routines?

6. What do you need to look after seasonally or several times a year?

7. When will you schedule your seasonal or other decluttering sessions?

8. What other major events will you declutter around?

Make your new routines into concrete plans, using this worksheet to help you with the other worksheets.

Three New Routines I Will Implement This Week

1. The first routine I will begin is

2. What would help me do this?

3. What will happen if I don't do this?

4. The second routine I will begin is

5. What would help me do this?

6. What will happen if I don't do this?

7. The third routine I will begin is

_____

8. What would help me do this?

_____

_____

9. What will happen if I don't do this?

_____

_____

_____

_____

Now use the following worksheets to make a plan for these new habits.

Morning Routine

1. What needs to be done in the morning?

2. The following acts or habits would help the rest of my day go smoothly . . .

3. As part of my morning routine, I will . . .

   (Use the habit stacking formula "After/Before [CURRENT HABIT], I will [NEW HABIT].")

Lunchtime Routine

1. What needs to be done at lunchtime?

2. The following acts or habits would help the rest of my day go smoothly . . .

3. As part of my lunchtime routine, I will . . .

   (Use the habit stacking formula "After/Before [CURRENT HABIT], I will [NEW HABIT].")

Evening Routine

1. What needs to be done in the evening?

2. The following acts or habits would help the rest of my day go smoothly . . .

3. As part of my evening routine, I will . . .

   (Use the habit stacking formula "After/Before [CURRENT HABIT], I will [NEW HABIT].")

Weekly Routines

1. What needs to be done weekly?

2. The following acts or habits would help my week go smoothly . . .

3. As part of my weekly routine, I will . . .

   (Use the habit stacking formula "After/Before [CURRENT HABIT] *or* on [SPECIFIC DAY], I will [NEW HABIT].")

Laundry Routine

1. The laundry that needs to be done in my home:

2. Can anyone else take over at least some of it? If so, who?

3. What will my new laundry routine look like?

	Who	When
Wash		
Dry		
Fold		
Put Away		

Spring Decluttering Checklist

Where we live, spring comes after an often long, gray winter. And the house—particularly the entryway, the yard, and the garage—definitely shows signs of wear and tear after all the salt and sand and melting snow. Even if you don't have such extreme seasonal weather fluctuations, spring is a good time for a refresh in your home. Here are some ideas for what to tackle in March or April, depending on the weather where you live.

☐ **Declutter your winter clothing and sports equipment.**
- Sort through and purge your winter clothes.
- Sort through and purge your winter sporting equipment.
- Make a list of anything you'll need to replace for next winter.
- Wash and put away the keepers for next winter.

☐ **Declutter your spring clothing and sports equipment (especially if you didn't last spring).**
- Sort through and purge your spring clothing.
- Sort through and purge your spring sporting equipment.
- Make a list of anything you'll need to get ASAP for this spring.
- Wash anything that needs washing and put it where you can access it easily for the season.

☐ **Declutter the fridge, freezers, and pantry (one at a time).**
- Empty everything out of the fridge, shelf by shelf and bin by bin. Immediately toss anything that's expired (empty jars and cans into the compost and recycle the containers if possible).
- Wipe down each shelf and bin.
- Sort everything as you go and then put things back where they belong. Add any new organizational and storage pieces that you noticed might help during the previous season.
- Finally, make note of anything that needs restocking.
- Look through the freezers and toss anything that has freezer burn or that has been there for way too long.
- Reorganize anything that's gotten messy or out of place. Add any new organizational and storage pieces that you noticed might help during the previous season.
- Finally, make note of anything that needs restocking.
- Next go through the pantry, tossing expired foods and tidying.
- Wipe down the shelves and return things to their proper homes. Add any new organizational and storage pieces that you noticed might help during the previous season.
- Finally, make note of anything that needs restocking.

☐ **Declutter the entryway and/or the mudroom.**
- Go through everyone's winter outdoor gear and get rid of anything that won't fit next season.
- If you store winter items in another location in the off-season, wash them and put them away.
- Get out the spring outerwear and go through it. Wash anything that needs washing.
- Make a list of any spring outerwear you will need to buy due to size or wear.
- Switch out your winter floor mats or rugs for spring ones. If you live somewhere with wicked winter weather where salt is used to melt ice and snow, be sure to clean your mats and rugs before you store them in the off-season.

☐ **Declutter the yard and outdoor toys/equipment.**
- Declutter your gardens by weeding, trimming, or pulling old dead plants or weeds.
- Get rid of any broken outdoor tools from winter or last spring, like shovels, rakes, etc.
- Make a list of outdoor tools, toys, or equipment you need for spring.
- Declutter your decor.
- Go through your linens and switch out heavier winter bedding for lighter bedding.
- Go through any winter bedding you didn't use or that got worn out this year and toss or donate it.
- Sort your lighter spring and summer bedding and donate or toss any you don't plan to use.
- Purge any spring or winter decor you didn't use or love—throw pillows, blankets, art, accessories. Someone else may love them even if you don't anymore.

☐ **Declutter the medicine cabinet.**
- Check your medicines and properly dispose of those that have expired.
- Make a list of any medications that you are out of or that you had to toss.
- Make sure your first aid kit is fully stocked in time for bike rides and scraped knees.

Summer Decluttering Checklist

The start of summer is a great time to make sure that everything is decluttered, prepped, and ready for some much-needed R&R. You can do the following in May or June, or whenever school lets out where you live.

☐ **Declutter your spring clothing and sports equipment.**
- Sort through and purge your spring clothes.
- Sort through and purge your spring sporting equipment.
- Make a list of anything you'll need to replace for next spring.
- Wash and put away the keepers for next spring.

☐ **Declutter your summer clothing and sports equipment (especially if you didn't last summer).**
- Sort through and purge your summer clothing.
- Sort through and purge your summer sporting equipment.
- Make a list of anything you'll need to get ASAP for this summer.
- Wash anything that needs washing and put it where you can access it easily for the season.

☐ **Declutter the fridge, freezers, and pantry (one at a time).**
- Empty everything out of the fridge, shelf by shelf and bin by bin. Immediately toss anything that's expired (empty jars and cans into the compost and recycle the containers if possible).
- Wipe down each shelf and bin.
- Sort everything as you go and then put things back where they belong. Add any new organizational and storage pieces that you noticed might help during the previous season.
- Finally, make note of anything that needs restocking.
- Look through the freezers and toss anything that has freezer burn or that has been there for way too long.
- Reorganize anything that's gotten messy or out of place. Add any new organizational and storage pieces that you noticed might help during the previous season.
- Finally, make note of anything that needs restocking.
- Next go through the pantry, tossing expired foods and tidying.
- Wipe down the shelves and return things to their proper homes. Add any new organizational and storage pieces that you noticed might help during the previous season.
- Finally, make note of anything that needs restocking.

☐ **Declutter school stuff.**
- Go through kids' backpacks and lunch boxes. Clean items that need cleaning. Toss broken items. There's nothing worse than forgetting about these all summer long and getting a moldy surprise before school starts again!
- Go through any homeschool or school supplies and toss broken items.
- Sort any homeschool books and return them to their shelves.
- Go through kids' school paperwork that has piled up and appropriately file memorabilia and any other necessary paperwork like report cards or homeschool portfolio items.
- Check kids' gym shoes for size and wear. Donate any that no longer fit, but that are in good condition. Toss the really worn-out ones.
- Do the same for any school uniforms.
- Make a list of items that will be needed for each kiddo come the end of summer so you're more prepared to go back-to-school shopping.

☐ **Declutter games, books, and puzzles.**
- Go through the games drawer or closet and get rid of any games that no one has played with for a few months, or games that have essential pieces missing.
- Sort through any puzzles and only keep the good ones.
- Go through the bookshelves (wherever they are in your house) and purge any books that no one reads or needs for reference. If your kids have outgrown books and you don't have any younger ones, keep a select few favorites and store them away in a memorabilia box or somewhere for later.

☐ **Declutter arts and crafts supplies.**
- Check your arts and crafts cupboard or drawers for broken crayons, dried-out markers, and too-small-to-be-useful paper scraps and get rid of them.
- Take inventory of what's left and make a list of any supplies you need.

☐ **Declutter summer outdoor toys and gear.**
- Sort through the smaller outdoor toys like pails and shovels, badminton racquets, pool toys, bubbles, and sidewalk chalk. Get rid of any broken items that are kicking around.
- Check bikes and bike helmets for any that have been outgrown or that are damaged. Donate anything useful and toss anything that's not. And why not pump up the bike tires and adjust the seat heights while you're at it?
- Make a list of any items you need, such as pool floaties or beach balls, and make time to go get them.

Fall Decluttering Checklist

The start of fall—either the unofficial start on Labor Day weekend in North America or the actual start of autumn in late September—is the time to once again clean up the yard, porch, and garage, particularly before winter. It's also a great time to look ahead to Thanksgiving and the holidays and declutter your fall decor, bakeware, and holiday gift-wrapping supplies.

☐ **Declutter your summer clothing and sports equipment.**
  - Sort through and purge your summer clothes.
  - Sort through and purge your summer sporting equipment.
  - Make a list of anything you'll need to replace for next summer.
  - Wash and put away the keepers for next summer.

☐ **Declutter your fall clothing and sports equipment (especially if you didn't last fall).**
  - Sort through and purge your fall clothing.
  - Sort through and purge your fall sporting equipment.
  - Make a list of anything you'll need to get ASAP for this fall.
  - Wash anything that needs washing and put it where you can access it easily for the season.

☐ **Declutter the fridge, freezers, and pantry (one at a time).**
  - Empty everything out of the fridge, shelf by shelf and bin by bin. Immediately toss anything that's expired (empty jars and cans into the compost and recycle the containers if possible).
  - Wipe down each shelf and bin.
  - Sort everything as you go and then put things back where they belong. Add any new organizational and storage pieces that you noticed might help during the previous season.
  - Finally, make note of anything that needs restocking.
  - Look through the freezers and toss anything that has freezer burn or that has been there for way too long.
  - Reorganize anything that's gotten messy or out of place. Add any new organizational and storage pieces that you noticed might help during the previous season.
  - Finally, make note of anything that needs restocking. And stock up a little extra on food if you live where the weather makes it harder to get out for last-minute missing ingredients.
  - Next go through the pantry, tossing expired foods and tidying.
  - Wipe down the shelves and return things to their proper homes. Add any new organizational and storage pieces that you noticed might help during the previous season.
  - Finally, make note of anything that needs restocking.

☐ **Declutter your decor.**
- Go through any summer bedding you didn't use or that got worn out this year and toss or donate it.
- Sort your fall and winter bedding and donate or toss any you don't plan to use.
- Purge any fall decor you don't use or love—throw pillows, blankets, art, or season-specific accessories, florals, and wreaths.
- Declutter for holiday guests.
- Go through your guest bedding and towels and toss or donate any you no longer want to use.
- Go through your tableware and purge anything you don't want or use anymore.
- Make a list of anything you need to replace before holiday guests are due to arrive.

☐ **Declutter bakeware.**
- Go through your bakeware and get rid of anything that's broken or damaged beyond repair or use.
- Make a list of anything that needs replacing and go get it in time to do your fall and holiday baking.

☐ **Declutter specific holiday items.**
- Sort and declutter your holiday gift-giving supplies like wrapping paper, gift bags, ribbons, tags, and cards. Toss any scraps that are too small.
- Make a list of gift-giving supplies that you need and make arrangements to order or purchase them soon so you're not in a rush come November or December.

Winter Decluttering Checklist

Winter brings on entirely new outdoor gear and, of course, all things holidays inside and outside your home. Make sure you're not wading through too much stuff or storing more than you need by decluttering these things at the beginning of the season. Your winter decluttering can be done in November or early December, depending on the holidays and weather where you live. For example, where I live (in Canada) we celebrate Thanksgiving in October. So, I start to plan and think about winter and the holidays by November 1. But I know that US Thanksgiving is in November, so fall season and celebrations seem to last longer there. Plan your winter decluttering accordingly.

☐ **Declutter your fall clothing and sports equipment.**
- Sort through and purge your fall clothes.
- Sort through and purge your fall sporting equipment.
- Make a list of anything you'll need to replace for next fall.
- Wash and put away the keepers for next fall.

☐ **Declutter your winter clothing and sports equipment (especially if you didn't last winter).**
- Sort through and purge your winter clothing.
- Sort through and purge your winter sporting equipment.
- Make a list of anything you'll need to get ASAP for this winter.
- Wash anything that needs washing and put it where you can access it easily for the season.

☐ **Declutter the fridge, freezers, and pantry (one at a time).**
- Empty everything out of the fridge, shelf by shelf and bin by bin. Immediately toss anything that's expired (empty jars and cans into the compost and recycle the containers if possible).
- Wipe down each shelf and bin.
- Sort everything as you go and then put things back where they belong. Add any new organizational and storage pieces that you noticed might help during the previous season.
- Finally, make note of anything that needs restocking.
- Look through the freezers and toss anything that has freezer burn or that has been there for way too long.
- Reorganize anything that's gotten messy or out of place. Add any new organizational and storage pieces that you noticed might help during the previous season.
- Finally, make note of anything that needs restocking.
- Next go through the pantry, tossing expired foods and tidying.

- Wipe down the shelves and return things to their proper homes. Add any new organizational and storage pieces that you noticed might help during the previous season.
- Finally, make note of anything that needs restocking and be sure you have enough food for winter emergencies if you live in a cold-weather climate.

☐ **Declutter holiday decorations.**

- As you begin to think about decorating the house for the holidays, go through all your holiday decor and toss broken or unwanted decor items.
- Make note of and buy any items you need or want to replace for the holidays this year.

Conclusion and a Few Final Thoughts

Phew! We have covered a lot in the last several pages, haven't we? Before we wrap up, I want to share a few final thoughts with you. First, here are a couple of simple rules to follow that may help you. I have a love-hate relationship with rules. I'm a bit of a rebel sometimes. But these rules will genuinely help you if you follow them.

The Four-Question Purchase Test

As I tell my Decorating Uncomplicated students when they're considering new decor purchases for their homes, *to avoid clutter in your home you should ask yourself a few questions before you buy anything for your home.* These questions will help you decide whether you actually need an item, or if you're buying it for unhealthy emotional reasons, or just because it's on sale. Don't buy anything else until you ask yourself these four questions:

1. Do I need it?
2. Do I adore it?

3. Do I have a place for it?
4. Am I willing to clean it up and put it away regularly?

Add these questions to a note in your phone, or type them out and print them. Then pull them out next time you find yourself tempted to buy something you may not need. **If you can't answer yes to all four questions, don't make that purchase!**

The One-In, One-Out Rule

This rule is the cardinal rule of professional organizers and minimalists everywhere. It's a rule that even I as a nonminimalist try to follow because it just makes sense for keeping your home clutter-free. Put very simply, the one-in, one-out rule means that whenever you bring one of something into the house, you have to get rid of something else. It's definitely best if the something you get rid of is related or similar to what you're bringing in, like a new throw pillow for an old throw pillow. This one item is like a drop in a bucket. But a little at a time, drop by drop, a bucket gets full of water—just as your house does with each item you bring into it. For a while, you don't notice. But eventually the bucket—and your house—is full to overflowing. If you're not careful, the bucket will spill over, making a soggy mess of everything. It can be very tempting to break this rule, telling yourself you'll get rid of one item "tomorrow." But tomorrow never comes. It's best to follow this rule to keep your home from feeling stuffed full again!

Be Thankful

Practice gratitude. Gratitude for what you have, no matter how little or how much. Gratitude for your home and the things in it. If you are grateful for things that you have, it will be much easier to feel content with your life and your home. Which will in turn help you to simplify and keep the clutter from accumulating in your life and home. If you need help with this, check out my first book, *Home Made Lovely*.

There is a whole chapter dedicated to helping you practice gratitude, plus a couple of simple exercises to make gratitude habitual. As we've learned, habits make all the difference.

Take Action

If you've only been reading and not acting up until now, I want to encourage you to get up off the couch right now and do something, *anything*, that will move the needle even just the tiniest bit in the right direction in your decluttering journey. "The journey starts with a single step—not with *thinking* about taking a step."[1] It will do your home and family zero good if you simply read through *The Clutter Fix* and then go on your merry way, never taking action to eliminate the clutter or get organized. *You have to actually start and then follow through.* Use the checklists and other tools. Write in the margins; highlight your favorite parts. Add the tabs (available in the printable bonus at HomeMadeLovely.com/tcfbonus) so you can reference specific steps and encouragement when needed.

It's about More Than Just the Stuff

By now you know that clutter isn't just about the stuff. It's about how we feel in our homes and how we are able to live out the lives and purposes God has called us to. It's mental and emotional, not just physical. It's about being good stewards of the time and resources God has given us. Remember the person you want to be. Remember why *you* want to have a clutter-free home. Follow the steps and the path I've outlined here, and you *will* make progress in your home, lovely. In Isaiah 32:18 God says, "My people will live in peaceful dwelling places, in secure homes, in undisturbed places of rest." You can't have that if your home is a cluttered mess. You need to declutter and organize for your health and well-being, and I genuinely hope that through *The Clutter Fix* I have been a help and a light for this part of your journey in your home here on earth. I hope that I've helped you to create a peaceful, secure place of rest for you and your family.

If you'd like to share your progress, use the hashtag #theclutterfix on social media along with your thoughts and photos. And if you'd like to keep in touch, please visit HomeMadeLovely.com to see all the resources I've collected there just for you. I can't wait to celebrate your lovely, decluttered home with you!

xo, Shannon

Notes

Introduction How to Use *The Clutter Fix*

1. Via a survey sent to the *Home Made Lovely* email list in 2020, with 241 responses.
2. Denise Ryan, "Tidying Up: The Psychology of Clutter and Why We're Now Cleaning It Up," *Vancouver Sun*, March 9, 2019, vancouversun.com/news/local-news /0309-clutter.
3. Denise Ryan, "Tidying Up."
4. Denise Ryan, "Tidying Up."
5. Mercari, "Study Reveals Clutter Epidemic Cause: 'Low Sell-Esteem,'" Cision PR Newswire, March 19, 2019, www.prnewswire.com/news-releases/study-reveals -clutter-epidemic-cause-low-sell-esteem-300814777.html.
6. Dana K. White, "Are You Too Emotionally Exhausted to Declutter?" *A Slob Comes Clean*, March 9, 2021, www.aslobcomesclean.com/2021/03/are-you-too -emotionally-exhausted-to-declutter.
7. Denise Ryan, "Tidying Up," emphasis mine.
8. Jeanne E. Arnold, Anthony P. Graesch, Enzo Ragazzini, and Elinor Ochs, *Life at Home in the Twenty-First Century: 32 Families Open Their Doors* (Los Angeles: Cotsen Institute of Archaeology Press, 2012), 25–26.
9. Dana K. White, "Are You Too Emotionally Exhausted to Declutter?"
10. Charles Duhigg, *The Power of Habit: Why We Do What We Do in Life and Business* (New York: Random House, 2014), 276.

Chapter 1 The 10-Day Decluttering Shortcut

1. "Mental Health Benefits of Decluttering," WebMD, October 25, 2021, www .webmd.com/mental-health/mental-health-benefits-of-decluttering.

Chapter 2 120 Things to Throw Away–Guilt-Free

1. Gretchen Rubin, "Eleven Myths of De-Cluttering," Gretchen Rubin, November 11, 2009, gretchenrubin.com/2009/11/eleven-myths-of-decluttering.

Chapter 3 Four Reasons to Simplify Your Home

1. Denise Ryan, "Tidying Up: The Psychology of Clutter and Why We're Now Cleaning It Up," *Vancouver Sun*, March 9, 2019, vancouversun.com/news/local-news /0309-clutter.

2. Sheri Steed, "Coming to Terms with Your Clutter Personality," Step-by-Step Declutter, www.step-by-step-declutter.com/clutter-personality.html.

Chapter 4 The Clutter Personalities

1. Chrissy Halton, quoted in Sheri Steed, "Coming to Terms with Your Clutter Personality," Step-by-Step Declutter, www.step-by-step-declutter.com/clutter-person ality.html.

2. Pixie Technology Inc., "Lost and Found: The Average American Spends 2.5 Days Each Year Looking for Lost Items Collectively Costing U.S. Households $2.7 Billion Annually in Replacement Costs," Cision PR Newswire, May 2, 2017, www.prnews wire.com/news-releases/lost-and-found-the-average-american-spends-25-days -each-year-looking-for-lost-items-collectively-costing-us-households-27-billion -annually-in-replacement-costs-300449305.html.

Chapter 6 How to Handle Sentimental Things

1. Sheri Bruneau, "What Can You Do about Sentimental Clutter Right Now," Get It Together, February 28, 2014, get-it-together.ca/warning-what-can-you-do-about -sentimental-clutter-right-now.

2. Kelly McGonigal, PhD, "Why It's Hard to Let Go of Clutter," *Psychology Today*, August 7, 2012, www.psychologytoday.com/ca/blog/the-science-willpower/201208 /why-it-s-hard-let-go-clutter.

3. Julia Brenner, "Marie Kondo, Take the Wheel: I'm Trying to Part with Senti-mental Clutter and It's HARD!" Apartment Therapy, April 3, 2017, www.apartment therapy.com/getting-rid-of-sentimental-clutter-even-when-its-really-really-hard -243228, emphasis mine.

4. Joanna Moorhead, "Marie Kondo: How to Clear Out Sentimental Clutter," *The Guardian*, January 14, 2017, www.theguardian.com/lifeandstyle/2017/jan/14/how -to-declutter-your-life-marie-kondo-spark-joy.

5. Joanna Gaines in Tara Bellucci, "Joanna Gaines Has a Smart Tip for Dealing with Sentimental Clutter," Apartment Therapy, December 30, 2017, www.apartment therapy.com/joanna-gaines-organizing-tip-sentimental-clutter-baby-clothes-25 4443.

6. Zawn Villines, "How to Help Someone Who Hoards," *Good Therapy*, June 21, 2014, www.goodtherapy.org/blog/how-to-help-hoarder-062114.

Chapter 7 How to Get Your Family on Board–or Not

1. Allie Casazza, "EP 092: Getting Your Unwilling Family on Board with Minimalism," Allie Casazza, January 9, 2019, alliecasazza.com/shownotes/092-2.

2. Keren Fortuna, Liora Baor, Salomon Israel, Adi Abadi, Ariel Knafo, "Attachment to Inanimate Objects and Early Childcare: A Twin Study," National Center for Biotechnology Information, May 22, 2014, www.ncbi.nlm.nih.gov/pmc/articles /PMC4033092.

3. Allie Casazza, "EP 092: Getting Your Unwilling Family on Board with Minimalism."

Chapter 8 Five Decluttering Mindset Hacks

1. Peter Walsh, quoted in Victor Maze, "20 Inspiring Quotes to Motivate You to Start Cleaning and Decluttering," Veranda, veranda.com/home-decorators/g3203 1382/decluttering-cleaning-quotes/?slide=8.

2. Hans Hofman, quoted in Victor Maze, "20 Inspiring Quotes to Motivate You to Start Cleaning and Decluttering," Veranda, veranda.com/home-decorators /g32031382/decluttering-cleaning-quotes/?slide=4.

3. James Clear, *Atomic Habits: An Easy & Proven Way to Build Good Habits & Break Bad Ones* (New York: Penguin Random House, 2018), 40.

4. Judi the Organizer, "10 Organizing Affirmations That Can Help You Get More Organized," Rescue My Space, January 16, 2018, Rescuemyspace.com/blog/2018 /1/16/10-organizing-affirmations-that-can-help-you-get-more-organized.

5. Joyce Meyer, *Battlefield of the Mind: Winning the Battle in Your Mind* (New York: Warner Books, 1995), 27.

6. Dr. Caroline Leaf, *Switch On Your Brain* product listing page, DrLeaf.com, drleaf .com/products/switch-on-your-brain.

Chapter 9 How to Purge and Organize Your Entire House in Seven Simple Steps

1. Steve McClatchy, quoted in "13 New Rules of Decluttering," *O, The Oprah Magazine*, March 2014, www.oprah.com/home/declutter-tips-organizing-strategies /10#ixzz2vmFJigoZ.

2. Emma Scheib, quoted in Victor Maze, "20 Inspiring Quotes to Motivate You to Start Cleaning and Decluttering," Veranda, www.veranda.com/home-decorators /g32031382/decluttering-cleaning-quotes/?slide=9.

Chapter 12 Step-by-Step, Room-by-Room Decluttering Guide

1. Libby Sander, "The Case for Finally Cleaning Your Desk," *Harvard Business Review*, March 25, 2019, hbr.org/2019/03/the-case-for-finally-cleaning-your-desk.

2. Whitmor Inc., Instagram, September 29, 2021, www.instagram.com/p/CUZ7U HHAoLJ.

Chapter 14 Routines and the Awesome Power of Habits

1. Jeff Olson, *The Slight Edge: Turning Simple Disciplines into Massive Success and Happiness* (Austin, TX: Greenleaf Book Group Press, 2005–2013), 235.

2. James Clear, "30 Days to Better Habits #1: How to Choose a Habit That Sticks," JamesClear.com, September 30, 2021.

3. James Clear, "30 Days to Better Habits #1."

4. James Clear, "How to Build New Habits by Taking Advantage of Old Ones," James Clear, jamesclear.com/habit-stacking.

5. James Clear, "How to Build New Habits."

6. James Clear, "How to Build New Habits."

Conclusion and a Few Final Thoughts

1. Jeff Olson, *The Slight Edge: Turning Simple Disciplines into Massive Success and Happiness* (Austin: Greenleaf Book Group Press, 2005–2013), 179.

Index

Author Bio

Shannon Acheson is a mostly self-taught designer, decorator, author of *Home Made Lovely*, and "all things home" coach. She believes home is the most important place on earth, and her passion is helping other mommas to love where they live and to use home to love on their friends, family, and neighbors.

Shannon has blogged at HomeMadeLovely.com since 2010 and has worked with some of the biggest brands in the home space—HomeSense, Ikea, Home Depot, Lowe's, Wayfair, and many more. Her work has been featured in magazines, online, and on television, including Oprah.com, *Steven and Chris*, *Farmhouse Style* magazine, *700 Club Canada*, and *Women's World* magazine.

Shannon's happy place is in the suburbs of Toronto, where she is a Homebody with a capital *H*, a Jesus girl, a happy wife to Dean, and a mom of three grown (or nearly grown) kiddos.

More from Shannon Acheson

How do you create a beautiful home without breaking the bank? Popular interior designer Shannon Acheson meets you right where you are and helps you share the peace of Christ with family members and guests through decluttering, decorating to suit your family's *real life*, and brushing up on hospitality with dozens of actionable ideas.

Home Made Lovely

 BETHANYHOUSE